ISBN: 9781290462051


Published by:
HardPress Publishing
8345 NW 66TH ST #2561
MIAMI FL 33166-2626

Email: info@hardpress.net
Web: http://www.hardpress.net

# THE HARRAP LIBRARY

*Further volumes will be announced later*

# KARMA ✤ ✤ ✤
## AND OTHER STORIES & ESSAYS
### ✤ ✤ BY LAFCADIO HEARN

# THE HARRAP LIBRARY

Lafcadio Hearn

# KARMA

AND OTHER STORIES &
ESSAYS ❧    ❧    ❧
BY LAFCADIO HEARN

LONDON: GEORGE G.
HARRAP & CO. LTD.
2-3 PORTSMOUTH ST. KINGSWAY
AND AT SYDNEY  ❧   ❧   ❧

*First published April* 1921

*Printed at* THE BALLANTYNE PRESS
SPOTTISWOODE, BALLANTYNE & CO. LTD.
*Colchester, London & Eton, England*

# EDITOR'S NOTE

THE stories and articles by Lafcadio Hearn in this volume are now collected in book form for the first time. They rank with his best work. The opening story, " Karma," is the most personal product from Hearn's pen, as he rarely took the public into his confidence. No doubt the ideal love described in this great tale was an experience of his own. The story originally appeared in *Lippincott's Magazine* for May, 1890.

" A Ghost "—a beautiful prose-poem—appeared in *Harper's Magazine* for December, 1889.

" The First Muezzin " was a work of great labour and love. In his letters to H. E. Krehbiel he makes numerous references to " The First Muezzin." It appeared in the New Orleans *Times-Democrat* in 1884. The sketch was considered to be lost to the world. I inquired from Mr Krehbiel about it; he discovered it in a scrap-book, which he kindly placed at my disposal.

" China and the Western World " appeared in the *Atlantic Monthly* for April, 1896. This article shows a keen insight into international relations, and is particularly timely to-day.

I wish to thank Captain Mitchell Mc-Donald, Hearn's friend and literary executor, for permission to reprint " Karma " and the four tales which complete this collection. I also wish to thank on behalf of Captain McDonald Messrs Harper Brothers for permission to include " A Ghost " in the present volume, and the Atlantic Monthly Publishing Company for permission to include " China and the Western World."

ALBERT MORDELL

# CONTENTS

# KARMA

# KARMA

WITH all her exceptional mental training, there was an almost childish ingenuousness in her every word and act,—a simplicity and directness of manner that invited every worthy confidence : yet he had never presumed to praise her. Behind that radiant girlishness, natural to her life as azure to sky, he knew some settled power,—some forceful intelligence to which a compliment would seem a rudeness. And, coerced to plainest frankness by his very sense of her personality, he found that it needed no little courage to make his declaration. For weeks he had attempted in vain to devise some way of softening the difficulty by preliminaries,—of giving some turn to conversation that might help him to approach the matter by gentle degrees. But she remained always so invulnerable to suggestion,—so strangely impregnable in her maidenly self-possession ! . . . To many lovers thus ill at ease, intuition tells the advantage of being alone with the adored girl somewhere beyond the shadow of walls,

—in some solitude where Nature softens hearts with her silence and her loveliness and perpetual prompting of what is tender and true,—a park, a wood, an umbraged lane. But to her, Nature and silence seemed to give larger power to awe him;—the splendid light itself seemed to ally with her against him. He lived near enough to be often with her; and they walked much together on quiet beautiful country-roads; and he never could find courage to do more than admire her by stealth, while conversing on subjects totally foreign to his thoughts. But each time more and more her charm bewildered him: the secret of ideal grace seemed to live in her,—that something in every motion and poise which is like melody made visible,—which makes you think you hear music when you see it.

With the passing of time his embarrassment only grew. Sometimes he would even find it impossible to maintain a sensible conversation,—conscious of nothing but his idolatry; answering questions vaguely, or not at all. . . . And at such a moment of his confusion, one day,—as they were returning

from a walk to her home,—she turned near
the little gate, and, looking into his face
with her archest smile, exclaimed :

—" Well, what is it ? Tell me all about
it. . . ."

## II

· Who does not know that luminous hour
of Love's illusion, when the woman beloved
seems not a woman,—never of earth, never
shaped of the same gross substance forming
man,—but a creature apart, unique, born of
some finer, subtler, pearlier life ? In her
the lover no longer beholds the real : she
has become to him so wonderful that he
cannot guard his secret,—that he must
speak of her so as to betray himself,—that
he feels anger when questioned friends
declare their inability to see those marvels
which he discerns in her. And then, with
this exquisite delirium of the senses, mysterious above aught else in the all-circling
mystery of life ;—with this wondrous be-
witchment, sung of since song found voice,
yet ever uninterpretable save as the working
magic of that Will wherefrom, as ether-

dartings from a sun-burning, are souls thrilled
out ;—with the astonishment of woman's
charm thus made divine,—the miracle of
her grace and purity of being,—there comes
to the lover a cruel sense of his own un-
worthiness. . . . What are you, O man !
poisoned with passions and knowledge of
evil, that you should think to mingle the
lucid stream of her life with the turbid
current of your own ? Were it less than
sacrilege to dream of it ? All limpid and
fleckless the azure of her thought : would
you make it grey ?—darken it ?—call into
it the cloudings that scathe with fire ? . . .
What are you, that she should make you her
chosen of all men,—accept her fate from
you ? . . . What are you, that she should
ever caress you,—suffer you to touch her, to
learn her thought, to seek the infinite in her
eyes, to know the sweet warm soft shock
of her kiss ?

Yet the illusion of her in those hours of
delicious madness when all the veins burn
with thirst of sacrifice for her sake ;—the
illusion of her during all the tense, fiery,

16

magnetic drawing of your life to hers with insensate longing to absorb it utterly and be therein impossibly absorbed,—to blend with it, to die for it : that illusion, however seeming-celestial, is less beautiful, infinitely less admirable, than the complex reality of her worth,—if she be indeed of the finer, rarer type of womanhood,—if she be indeed one of those marvellously-specialized human flowers that bloom only in the higher zones of aspirational being,—even at the verge of God's snow-line. . . . Have you ever thought what she truly is,—this perfumed chalice-blossom stored with all sweetness of humanity ?—have you ever dreamed what she is worth ?

. . . For all the myriads of the ages have wrought to the making of her. Æons of struggle and blood and tears are the price of her. And in that she is good,—because of the soul-sweetness of her,—is she not the utmost yet-possible expression of divinity working through man ? . . . Think you what her sweetness means,—the free beauty of her mind,—the tenderness of her,—the sensitive exquisiteness of her being ! It signifies so much more than she . . . ! It means the whole history of love striving against hate, aspiration against pain, truth against ignorance, sympathy against pitilessness. She,—the soul of her!—is the ripened passion-flower of the triumph. All the heroisms, the martyrdoms, the immolations of self,—all strong soarings of will through fire and blood to God since humanity began,—conspired to kindle the flame of her higher life.

And yet, perhaps, she is willing to be yours!

Viewlessly your being has become slowly interorbed with hers;—each life is secretly seeking union with the other through interweaving of wishes unconfessed. Within her charming head are thoughts and dreams and beliefs about you. Something shadowy,—an emanation of you, an illusion,—has entered into that limpid life, and tinted all its thinking, as clearest water is tinted by one touch of eosin, and flushes through with rose-colour of dawn. Her blood has learned of you in the blind sweet pink chambers of her life,—quickens its throbbing at the echo of your step, at the sound of your voice . . . even at the remembrance of your face. In sleep she speaks to you,—to your Eidolon,—to the shadow of you apotheosized by the wondrous mirroring of her girl's-love. Her wishes are of you; her plans are shapen for you : some thought you uttered has been utilized in that secret splendid architecture of faith being builded within her dainty brain. Was it real enough, strong enough, flawless enough to serve for so holy a use ?—or was it sleazy and false,— ready to yield at the first unlooked-for pressure, and bring down with its breaking all the charming gracious fabric innocently confided to its support ?

—" Have I the generous skill to make her happy ? . . . Have I the methods of wealth to keep want far from her ? . . . Have I the force to wrestle with the world for her,— and win ? . . . Am I strong enough to protect her from all harm ? . . . Shall I be able to provide for her and for her children in all things, should death come suddenly to take me away ? " . . . Are these all the

19

honest questions that you ask yourself?
And having asked, and found the power to
cry out *Yes* to every asking, do you think
you have asked enough? . . . Nay! such
questions are babble to other questions
which selfishness or ignorance may have
prevented you from asking, but which it
remains your duty to demand: your duty
to her,—your duty to the future,—your duty
to mankind,—your duty to the Supreme
Father of all life and love.

. . . For what purpose was she formed?
. . . Surely to be loved. . . . But for what
purpose loved? Ah! never for yours alone!
Only for the divine purpose came she into
being,—this Love-Kindler,—foam-born out
of life's sea-bitterness under the lashing of
all the Winds of pain. And through her,
as through each so-far-perfected form, the
eternal Will is striving to bring souls out of
Night into the splendour of that time when
the veil between divine and human shall
have been taken away.

In her beauty is the resurrection of the
fairest past;—in her youth, the perfection of

the present;—in her girl-dreams, the promise of the To-Be. . . . Million lives have been consumed that hers should be made admirable; countless minds have planned and toiled and agonized that thought might reach a higher and purer power in her delicate brain;—countless hearts have been burned out by suffering that hers might pulse for joy;—innumerable eyes have lost their light that hers might be filled with witchery;—innumerable lips have prayed for life that hers might be kissed. . . .

 And can you dare to love her without ghostly fear?—without one thought of all the hopes, strivings, sacrifices, sufferings which created her?—without terror of your weird responsibility to the past and its dead pains,—to all those vanished who laboured that she might see the light? Numberless they may have been; yet how unspeakably vaster the multitude of possibilities involved by her single slender existence! Not to the sacrificial past alone are you responsible, but to the mysterious To-Come also and much more,—and to that Unknowable likewise, working within and beyond all time,—

that Will which is Goodness. . . . Through her young heart throbs rosily the whole God-Future : its love, its faith, its hope are seeking there to quicken,—all flower-wise folded up in the bud of her exquisite life. . . .

### III

. . . She did not appear surprised when he uttered his wish : she only became a little serious,—and met his gaze without one sign of shyness, as she made answer :—

—" I do not yet know. . . . I am not sure you love me."

—" Oh, could you but try me ?—what would I not do ! . . ."

Placid as sculpture her face remained, while her fine silky-shadowed eyes observed, as with a curious doubting sympathy,—the passionate eagerness of his look.

—" But I do not approve of those words," she said. " If I thought you meant all that is in them, I might not like you."

—" Why ? " he queried, in surprise.

—" Because there are so many things one should not do for anybody. . . . Would you do what you suspected or knew to be wrong for the purpose of pleasing me ? "

He was afraid to answer at once ;—but she read his thought in the quick hot blush that followed it,—and the blush pleased her more than his words.

—" I do not really know," she resumed, after a moment's silence,—moving, as she spoke, to pluck a flower from the neighbouring hedge,—" I do not know yet whether I ought to allow myself to like you."

. . . Her expression of doubt made him happy,—suddenly, wildly happy. His heart filled full almost to breaking with the delight of her words : yet he could imagine nothing to say or do. He feared this strange girl,—feared her as much as he loved her. . . . For fully a minute she played with the flower in silence,—and that minute seemed to him very long. The flower photographed itself upon his brain with a vividness that remained undiminished to the day of his death. It was a purple aster. . . .

—" Let me tell you,"—she continued at last, looking straight into his eyes with her clear keen sky-grey frankness,—" let me tell

you what to do. . . . Go home now : then,—
as soon as you feel able to do it properly,—
write out for me a short history of your life ;
—just write down everything you feel you
would not like me to know. Write it,—and
send it. . . ."

—" And then ? " he asked, as she paused a
little.

—" And then I shall tell you whether I
will marry you,"—she finished, resolutely.
. . . " Now, good-bye ! "

—" But," he persisted, clinging almost
desperately to the slender hand extended,—
" you will believe me . . . ? "

—" How believe you ? . . . If I did not
think I could believe you," she answered,
surprised into sternness, and at once with-
drawing her hand,—" I should already have
told you very plainly, No ! "

—" Only that I love you," he explained.
She only smiled and repeated,—
—" Good-bye ! "

# KARMA

## IV

*... " Write out for me a short history of your life ; ... write down everything you feel you would not like me to know. ... "*

So easy a task it seemed that he hurried homeward filled with the impulse to do it at once,—wondering at the length of the way in his impatience to begin. ... *" Then I shall tell you whether I will marry you. ... "* Something joyous filled his whole being with lightness and force,—the elixir of hope! He thought of the duty imposed on him as almost pleasurable,—without knowing why. ... Perhaps because in reviewing our own faults we are wont to compassionate ourselves as victims of circumstances, and to betray our weaknesses to a friend is therefore to invite the consolation of sympathy with our own self-pity. ...

But this eagerness was of the moment only, —the moment of nervous reaction succeeding suspense, before he had yet time to think. In a little while it passed away under the influence of a growing conviction that the undertaking was serious enough to decide his whole life. A single phrase might lose him incomparably more than he had gained,—might even condemn him irrevocably. And the indulgent manner of her own words recurred to him as a gentle caution against impulsiveness :—" *As soon as you feel able to do it properly.*"

And ere reaching home he had ceased to feel at all confident. Unexpectedly,—one after another,—there had recurred to him certain incidents of his career as a young man which could not be written down with ease. The simple recollection of them came with a little sharp shock : a young man's follies, of course, but follies that could not be recorded without extreme care of expression. . . .                                    .

. . . " *Everything you feel you would not like me to know.* . . .'' Surely she could not have understood the full possible significance of her command ! Neither could she suppose, unless most strangely innocent, that men were good like women ! . . . But what if she could and did suppose it ? In that event, the faintest reference to certain passages of his life must cause her cruel surprise. . . .

26

" *Everything you feel you would not like me to know. . . .* " All or nothing !

And he found himself almost startled by this first definite comprehension of the duty to be performed,—the problems to be solved, —the delicate subtle severity of that moral test he had so lightly welcomed as a relief from love's incertitude.

## V

To make a rough draft of all that ought to be written, and then amend, refine, compress, correct, and recopy,—had first appeared to him the readiest way of obeying her wishes. But subsequent reflection led him to believe that such a method involved temptation to vanity of style, conceit of phrase,—general insincerity of expression. With his freshly-acquired right to the hope of winning her, there began to stir and expand within him a sense of gratitude unspeakable to the giver, and a new courage of trustfulness likewise, which momentarily conquered his doubts. No : it would be more loyal to write down

27

each fact as it came to memory,—simply, bravely, candidly,—and send her the original record in its plain spontaneous sincerity. . . . For a little while he felt himself exalted with zeal of frankness,—with high resolve to master his sensitiveness,—to overrule any secret wish to appear better than he was.

. . . But after having remained more than an hour at his desk, he found this second courage of purpose also fail him. The record of his childhood and early youth,—even the detailed narrative of his first struggle in the world of adult effort, with a heart still fresh, timid, loving,—bewildered by the great stirring about and beyond it, like some cage-born creature loosed in a wood,—all this had not been difficult to write. There was nothing in it that he could not feel willing she should know. But thereafter the course of his duty seemed fraught with peril ; and all his former doubts and fears came thronging back to haunt him. It was not going to prove so easy to make as he had for one foolish moment presumed to believe,—this confession of sins ! . . .

And the dismay of difficulties unforeseen,

28

—the fear of making known to her, even by intimation, matters which he had so often recounted to friends without a thought of shame,—began to excite within him an unfamiliar indefinable feeling of moral bewilderment. How strangely, how violently such incidents shifted their colour when brought, even by fancy, into the atmosphere of luminous, passionless purity which enveloped her! Could it be possible that he had never before looked at them save in artificial light,—under the delusive glare of some factitious morality?

. . . *"Everything you feel you would not like me to know. . . ."* Yet why falter? Surely the sweet command itself implied the promise of all possible pardon! . . . And, after all, the only feasible way of obeying it would be that which he had thought of at the outset,—to set everything down bluntly, and then reshape the whole,—ameliorate the form.

. . . But even thus the task exacted more painful thinking than he had been able to foresee. So many impressions had become blurred or effaced in his remembrance!— there were links missing between incidents ;

29

—there were memories of acts without recollection of precedents and impulses,—without record of those circumstances which alone could mitigate their aspect of perversity. . . . Yes, it was true that he did not wish to appear any better than he was ;—but, in her eyes, at least, he dare not suffer himself to seem worse. . . . Slowly and carefully—in the pauses of his nervous pacing up and down the room for hours,—he elaborated another page . . . a page and a half, of letter-paper. Then he read over all that he had written.

His face burned at the mere thought of those lines being seen by her. " Never ! " he cried out aloud to himself,—" never could I send her that ! " . . . It would have to be modified—totally modified in some way. Yet to change it enough,—without insincerity,—without positive untruthfulness,—seemed almost impossible. And this was what he had thought himself able to do immediately ! . . . Could she have divined that it would not be easy to do, when she had said,—so slowly and distinctly in that soft penetrating voice of hers,—"*As soon as you feel able* " ? . . .

. . . Darkness found him still at his desk ;
and the task did not seem to him even fairly
begun : all its difficulties appeared to multiply
and to make more and more confusion in his
mind the longer he thought about them.
He lighted his lamp, and worked on, hour
after hour,—struggling with the stony hard-
ness of statements which no skill of honest
verbal chemistry could soften,—trying to
remodel sentences already rewritten a score
of times. . . . It was long past midnight
when he rose from his desk overweary, and
resigned his writing to seek repose,—utterly
astounded at the result of this strange obli-
gation to testify against himself in the secret
high court of honour,—to estimate the moral
value of his life by the simple measure of one
sweet girl's idea of goodness. . . .

## VI

He laid himself down to rest ; but the cool
peace of sleep would not come : his thought,
heated to pain by all the emotions of the day,
still burned on,—flaming and smouldering
by turns. Sometimes he saw her eyes, her

smile—fancied he could hear her voice ;—then his unfinished manuscript seemed always to rise up magnified between them,—like a great white written curtain wavering soundlessly, with ominous distortions of meaning in every undulation. Then he would try to review all that he had penned, only to remember involuntary errors or to detect insincerities compelled by the vain effort to make some compromise between absolute frankness and positive deceit,—until his thought would drift back, undirected by any purpose, into the past. But always, sooner or later, he would find himself sharply recalled as by a sudden fear to the remembrance of the present,—of her,—of her last words, —and the white nightmare of his unfinished confession.

. . . Repeatedly he strove to quell this mental agitation, to win back internal calm by reasoning with that once more self-asserting conscience, now recognizably aggressive, which had been so long dumb that he believed it appeased when it was only sullen,—reduced to silence by some false and subtile casuistry, but never conciliated. He sought to find excuses, apologies, explanations for his faults,—marshalling in memory all mitigating circumstances of each yielding to guilty impulse,—endeavouring to convince himself of the insignificance of an act by optimistic judgment of its consequences. Inexperience was so blind ; —youth could delude so cruelly ! . . . And yet were not many men,—men like him,— made wiser and better by their early follies, stronger by their weaknesses ?—souls tempered into self-mastery through error and regret, as steel through fire and water ? . . . Was he not of these ? Might she not so absolve him,—suffer him to love her ? Dare he not hope that she would pardon him all that he could fully forgive himself ?—and surely there was nothing he could not forgive himself . . . except—

—*Except* . . . ! Ah ! there he had been more than weak, more than foolish, worse than selfish ! . . . In that instance at least, conscience had confuted all argument,— scorned all consolation. It was not an error : it was crime, — unmistakable wickedness. No studied elimination of details could make it otherwise appear in that which he had to write. He had known that fault so well for what it was that he had trained his mind never to dwell upon it,—disciplined his recollection to avoid it. . . . And with the burning memory of it, there suddenly revived other kindred remembrances of shame and pain : things before forgotten, because of his long effort to efface from the mental chart of his life, a whole zone of years. But now, every marking thus obliterated,—all the reefs and shoals and drifting wrecks of old storm-spaces,—had risen into visibility again. . . . Never, never could he tell her of these ! . . .

Then he must lose her,—lose her irrevocably ! And losing her, what could life be worth to him ? To lose her would be to lose himself,—his higher self,—all the nobility of that new being into which his love for her had lifted him up. True it was that she had ever seemed placed by her loftier nature beyond his reach ;—that he had entered into the pure repose about her, feeling as an intruder,—as one having wandered unbidden with raiment blood-besprinkled into some

34

seraphic peace, and trembling for the moment
of banishment, yet with unhallowed feet
held fast by strangest spell of bliss. . . . And
nevertheless was she not all in all his com-
plement,—light to his shadowing, snow to
his fire, strength to his weakness ?—a nature
evolved with marvellous appositeness for
union with his own ? Not that he could
presume to deem himself thus worthy, but
that she might render him so much more
worthy by loving him ! . . . To lose her ? . . .
All that his aspiration had ever imaged of
ideal human goodness, all that his heart had
ever hungered for, responded to her own
dear name !—nay ! before her he found himself dazzled as by divinity, so transcendently
were all his dreams surpassed. . . . To lose
her ? He alone, out of all the thousands
destined to seek in vain,—the myriads deluded
by hope of winning the Woman never to be
known,—he only had been fated to find his
ideal. Had he then found her only to lose
her for ever ?

—"*Everything you feel you would not like
me to know.*" . . . Did she—could she—
suspect there were incidents of his life which

35

he dared not write ? Had she simply decided to checkmate his wooing by forcing him to accept a sort of moral chess-game of which she had foreseen every possible move from the beginning ? . . . The pitiable suspicion perished in a moment ; but there sprang up at once in the place of it his first impulse to positive insincerity. Could he not deceive her ?—might he not dissemble ? Over and over again he asked himself the question,— justifying and condemning his weakness by turns ; and each time her words flashed back to him :—" *Would you do what you thought or felt to be wrong to please me ?* " . . . "Yes, I would !" he once passionately cried out in answer ; and then felt himself blush again in the dark for the cowardice of the acknowledgment. . . . But even though he would, he knew that he could not. Even were he to write a lie, he could not meet her and maintain it, with her eyes upon his face : they had uttermost power over him— power as of life and death,—those fine grey sweet mesmeric eyes !

. . Then what was he to do ? Confess himself a criminal by praying her to forgo the test after having begged her to prove him? . . . Ask her — ask Truth's own Soul!—to take him to herself with that black falsehood in his life? . . . Write her all,—and die? . . . Write nothing, and disappear for ever from the world to which she belonged? . . .

## VII

Yet why this intensifying dread,—like the presage of a great pain? . . . Why had he always feared that slight girl even while loving her?—feared her unreasoningly, like a supernatural being,—measuring his every thought in the strange restraint of her presence? . . . How imperfect his love, if perfect love casteth out fear! Imperfect by so much as his own nature was imperfect; but he had loved less perfectly with never a thought of fear. . . . By what occult power could she make him thus afraid? Perhaps it was less her simple beauty, her totally artless grace, which made her unlike all other women, than the quiet settled consciousness of this secret force. Assuredly

37

those fine grey eyes were never lowered before living gaze : she seemed as one who might look God in the face. . . . Men would qualify such sense of power as hers, ' strength of character ' ; —but the vague term signified nothing beyond the recognition of the power as a fact. Was the fact itself uninterpretable ? —a mystery like the mystery of life ?

## VIII

. . . But imperceptibly, all self-questioning weakened and ceased. Weariness began to flood his thought,—like some grey silent rising tide, spreading and drowning. Ideas slowly floated up, half-formed,—soft and cold. . . . Then darkness,—and a light in the darkness that illumined *her*,—and the sense of some strange interior unknown to him.

He saw her in that filmy light, imponderably poised, with ghostliest grace made visible through some white vapour of veils ; —the glossiness of her arms uplifted for the braiding of her hair, seeming the radiance of some substance impossible,—like luminous

38

ivory. And this soft light that orbed and bathed her, held some odorous charm,—thin souls of flowers,—faint, faint perfume of dream-blossoms. And he knew that she was robing for her wedding with him.

He stood beside her : the soft spheral light touched him. . . . All around them was a great pleasant whispering,—the whispering of many friends assembled. He looked into the penumbra beyond her, and saw smiling faces that he knew. Some were of the dead ; but it seemed right they should be there. Would they smile thus —would they whisper so kindly—*if they knew* . . . ?

And there arose within him a weird interior urging to tell all ;—and that knowledge of self-unworthiness which had haunted him in other hours, suddenly returned upon him with the enormity of a nightmare,—irresistible, appalling,—like a sense of infinite crime. Then he knew that he must tell her all.

And he began to speak—to confess to her each hidden blemish of his life,—passionately watching her face,—feeling for her

39

power to forgive,—fearfully seeking to learn
if her pure hate of evil might exceed the
measure of her sound sweet human love.
. . . Yet now she seemed not human : all
transfigured she had become ! And those
white shapes enfolding her were surely
never bridal veils, but vapoury wings that
rose above her golden head, and swept down
curving to her feet.

. . . Angel !—but with a woman's heart !
. . . For she only smiled at his words, at
his fears, with compassionate lovingness,—
with tenderness as of maternal indulgence
for the follies of a child. . . . Ah ! but all
his follies had not been trivial ;—there were
others she never could forgive. . . .

But still she listened,—smiling as one
hearing nothing new, with sympathy of
strange foreknowledge,—all the while with
supplest slender arms uplifted, weaving her
marvellous hair.

And he knew that all those there assembled
heard his every syllable ;—yet he could not
but speak on,—charging himself with crimes
he had never wrought,—calumniating his
life, even as victims of inquisitorial torture

shrieked out self-accusation of impossible sins. But always, always she laughed forgiveness,—and those in the circling shadow likewise ;—and he heard them commending him,—commending his sacrifice, his sincerity, his love of her : infinitely indulgent for him.

Yet the more they praised him, the greater became his fear of making one last avowal,— of uttering that which was the simple truth. For a weird doubt seized upon him,—a doubt of their meaning ; and with the growing of it, all seemed treacherously to change. . . . And the faces of the dead were sinister ;—the murmuring hushed : even she no longer smiled. . . .

He would have whispered it to her alone ; but ever as he sought to lower his voice, more piercing it seemed to sound,—cutting through the stillness with frightful audibility, like the sibilation of a possessing spirit. . . . And then, in mad despair, ceasing to hope for secrecy, he uttered it recklessly, —vociferated it,—reiterated it, crashed it into their hearing with the violence of a blasphemy.

All vanished !—there was only darkness about him, the darkness of real night. . . . Still trembling with the terror of his dream he heard his own heart beat, and some slow distant steeple-bell strike out the hour of four.

## IX

Not through that restless night alone, but through many nights succeeding to weariest days of self-questioning and self-recording, conscience unrelentingly revenged every past repudiation of its counsel. Day after day, he would tear up a certain page and begin it afresh, but each time only to hear that vindictive inner voice make protest,—deny his right to any palliating word. And when everything else had been written, the inexorable Censor still maintained, still refused to attenuate, the self-proscription penned upon that page. Neither by finest analysis of motives and circumstances converging to the fault, nor by any possible deduction out of consequences, could the blackness of the fact be diminished : the great blot of it, spreading either way, strangely discoloured the whole. . . . Without that page his manuscript could offer at the very worst only a record of follies hurtful to none so much as to himself;—with it,—read through the smirch of it,—no other error avowed could seem innocuous enough to demand her absolution.

And the days wheeled away, filing off by weeks;—and a new anxiety began to shape for him. The mere prolongation of his silence was betraying him. Already she might have divined his moral cowardice, and decided against him. Before this imminent menace of what he feared most, he found himself finally terrified to a resolve,— as one leaps into flood from fire. He turned one morning to his manuscript for the decisive time, re-read once more the ever-scored page, feverishly copied it, folded it up with the rest, enveloped and addressed the whole; and then, feeling the inevitable danger of another moment's hesitation, he hurried out and dropped the manuscript into the nearest letter-box.

## X

Then he became appalled at what he had done. . . . Seldom does the whole potential meaning of a doubtful act consent to reveal itself while the act is yet only contemplated ; and that sudden expansion of significance which it assumes immediately upon accomplishment, may form the most painful astonishment of a lifetime. . . .

Oh ! the subtle protean treachery of words on paper !—words that, only spoken, seemed so harmless ;—that once embodied and coiled in writing, change nature and develop teeth to gnaw the brain that gave them visible form ! The viewless fluttering spoken word is thrice pleaded for : by the tone which is the heart of it, and its best excuse for being,— by the look which accompanies it,—by the circumstance which evokes it. But incarnate it with a single quivering dash of the pen,— and lo ! the soulless, voiceless, gelid impersonality of a reptile. Still, you are so far conscious only of its chilling ugliness ;— you do not know its dumb cruelty : it is feigning innocuousness because its life is

44

yet at your mercy,—because it has not ceased to be your slave. The price of its manumission is a postage-stamp. Release it, and it will writhe through all your soul to tear and to envenom. Then you will be powerless to prevail against it : freedom will have given it the invulnerability of air !

. . . And words that might have been spared in sentences that should have been reconsidered,—with what multiformity of ghastliness they now swarmed back to madden him,—biting into memory ! How had he failed to discern their whole evil capability,— to understand, while it was not yet too late, their sinister power of shifting colour according to position, according even to the eye that looked upon them ? Under what hue would they reveal themselves to her ? . . . And not one could now, or ever again, be changed. He had flung his missive into the machinery of government ; and already, doubtless, by steam and iron, it was being whirled to its destination !

Yes !—there was still a forlorn hope !

45

What if he should telegraph to have the manuscript returned unopened ? . . . But again,—what would she infer from such a message ? . . . A new confusion of doubts and fears and desperate conflicting impulses followed. But the dread of her inference yielded at last to the vividly terrible menace of lines that he had written,—even becoming more frightfully visible in remembrance,— visions that left him soul-steeped in a fire-agony of shame ! . . . He rushed out into the street,—hurried to the telegraph-office. As he entered it, he glanced almost instinctively at the mockingly placid face of the clock,—and started, with a sensation at his heart as of falling in dreams. . . . Time often passes with a rapidity that seems malevolent when the emotions are in turmoil. . . . It was too late to telegraph. The envelope had already, in all likelihood, been opened by her own hands !

## XI

It was done,—for ever done! . . . He had cast the die of his own fate. And the absolute conviction of his further helplessness restored him to comparative calm,—subdued that passion of emotional pain which it had seemed to him that he could endure no longer and live. . . .

Could she forgive him? Might she not be merciful? Might she not have some such intuition of the nature of human weakness as would impel her to hold him pardonable in view of the contrition he had so earnestly expressed? And might he not place some hope in her strange capacity of independent judgment,—of estimating character and action by standards wholly at variance with common opinion?

Perhaps. . . . But in her sublime indifference to conventional beliefs, there was always manifest a moral confidence steady as the steel of a surgeon. . . . And there came to him the first vague perception of why he feared her,—of what he feared in her: a penetrative dynamic moral power that he felt without comprehending. . . . The idea of that power applied to the analysis of his confession, brought down his heart again.

There were three—only three fearful things she might do : simply condemn him by her silence ; write him her refusal ; or summon him to hear from her own lips that all was over. And the last possibility seemed the most to be dreaded. Why ? . . . Was it because of an intuition that he might hear something more terrible than her ' No ' ? . . . He remembered strange hours of his life when the reality of an occurrence feared had proven infinitely more painful than the imagining,—though fancy had been fore-warned and strained to prepare him for the very worst. The imagined worst had never been the worst : there were fathomless abysses of worse behind it.

And the simple word, ' Come,'—solitary and imperative,—in a note received two days later, suddenly thickened and darkened within him this indefinite fear of an unimaginable worse. So feels the prisoner, long waiting for his doom,—when the hammering has ceased to echo in the night,—and the iron doors grate open to grey dawn,—and the Mask says, " Come ! "

## XII

. . . As he opened the door of the apartment in which they had been wont to meet, and the faint familiar fragrance that seemed a part of her life, smote softly to his brain,— he saw her there, already risen, as one who knew his footstep, to take from some locked drawer an envelope he instantly recognized. The mere deliberate swift manner of the act prepared him, before he could see her face, for the absence of the sweet smile with which she had always greeted him. She neither asked him to be seated, nor approached to offer him her hand, but walked directly to the hearth where a bright wood fire was leaping.

—"Do you wish me to burn this?" she asked, with the missive in her hand, and her eyes flashing to his face. Her voice had the ring of steel !

—" Yes," he responded, almost in a whisper.

. . . Only one moment he saw her eyes,—for he turned away his own ; but that single strong glance seemed to flame cold into his life like some divine lightning,—incinerating the uttermost atom of his hope,—consuming the last thin wrapping of his pride, like a garment of straw. For the first time he knew himself spiritually stripped before a human gaze ;—and with that knowledge outvanished in shame all the weakness of his passion,—all the sense-hunger that is love's superstition. He stood before her as before God, —morally naked as a soul in painted dreams of the Judgment Day. . . .

She tossed the written paper to the fire, and watched it light up with a little flapping sound ; while he stood by,—fearing what her next word might be. As the flame sank, an air-current wafted and whirled the weightless ash up out of sight. . . . A moment passed, and it came crumbling down again, by flakes, that fluttered back like moths into the blaze.

—" You say the woman is dead ? " she questioned at last, in a very quiet voice,—still looking in the fire.

He knew at once to which page of his confession she referred, and made answer :—

·—" It is almost five years since she died."

—" And the child ? "    ·

—" The boy is well."

—" And . . . your . . . *friend ?* " She uttered the words with a slow, strange emphasis,—as of resolve to master some repulsion.

—" He is still there,—in the same place."

Then turning to him suddenly, she exclaimed,—with a change of tone cold and keen as a knife :—

—" And when you wrote me *that,* you had really forced yourself to believe I might condone the infamy of it ! . . . "

He attempted no response,—so terribly he felt himself judged. He turned his face away.

—" Assuredly you had some such hope," she resumed ;—" otherwise you could not have sent me that paper. . . . Then by what moral standard did you measure me ?

51

—was it by your own ? . . . Certainly your imagination must have placed me somewhere below the level of honest humanity,—below the common moral watermark ! . . . Conceive yourself judged by the world—I mean the real world,—the world that works and suffers ; the great moral mass of truthful, simple, earnest people making human society ! Would you dare to ask their judgment of your sin ? Try to imagine the result ;— for by even so easy a test you can immediately make some estimate of the character of what you confessed to me,—as a proof of your affection ! . . . "

Under the scorn of her speech he writhed without reply. And kindled by it, as fire by a lens of ice, there began to burn within him a sense of shame to which all his previous pain was nothingness,—an anguish so incomparable that he wondered at his power to live. . . . For there are moments of weirdest agony possible in the history of natures that have not learned the highest lesson of existence,—strange lightning-glimpses of self-ability to suffer,—astonishments of moral perception suddenly expanded beyond all limit preconceived,—like immense awakenings from some old dreaming, some state of soul-sleep long mistaken for truth of life. . . . So sometimes, to unripened generous hearts, flash the first fearful certitudes of an ethical law stronger than doubt or dogma,—the supreme morality at once within and without all creeds, beyond and above all scepticisms. He was of those for whom its revelation comes never save through pain,—as certain tardy fruits are sweetened by frost ; — she was of those born into goodness, inheriting truth as a divine instinct. And by that instinct she knew him as it had not been given him to know himself. . . .

—" You think me cruel," she resumed, after a brief silence. " Oh, no !—I am not cruel ; I am not unjust. I have made allowances. I wished you to come and see me because in every line of your avowal I found evidence that you did not know the meaning of what you wrote,—that even your shame was merely instinctive,—that you had no manly sense of the exceptional nature of your sin. And I do not intend to

53

leave you in the belief that so deadly a wrong can be dismissed,—least of all by yourself,—as a mere folly, something to be thought about as little as possible. For the intrinsic vileness of it is in no manner diminished, either by your cheap remorse or by your incapacity to understand it except as a painful error. My friend, there are errors which Nature's God never fails to punish as crimes. Sometimes the criminal may escape the penalty ; but some one else must bear it. Much that is classed as sin by the different codes of different creeds, may not be sin at all. But transcendent sin,—sin that remains sin for ever in all human concepts of right and wrong,—sin that is a denial of all the social wisdom gained by human experience ;—for such sin there is no pardon, but atonement only. And that sin is yours ; and God will surely exact an expiation."

—" Is it not enough to lose you ? " he sobbed,—turning at last his gaze, all fevered by despair, to seek her face.

—" By no means ! " she answered, with terrible composure. " That is no expiation !

54

But what may prove at best a partial expiation, I now demand of you. I demand it in God's name. I demand it in your own behalf. I demand it also as my right . . . My right !—*mine !*—for you have wronged me also by the consequences of that crime, O my friend !—and you owe me the reparation ; and I demand it of you—yes !—to the last drop of the dregs of the bitterness of it ! . . . "

Her merciless calm had passed : she now spoke with passion,—and the force of her passion appalled him. Never before had he seen her face flushed by anger.

—" You will go, my friend, to that man whom you wronged,—that man who still lives and loves under the delusion of your undying lie,—and you will tell him frankly, plainly, without reserve, what you have dared to confess to me. You will ask him for that child, that you may devote yourself to your own duty ; and you will also ask how you may best make some reparation. Place your fortune, your abilities, your life, at that man's disposal. Even should he wish to kill you, you will have no right to resist. But I would rather,—a thousand times rather you should find death at his hands, than to know that the man I might have loved could perpetrate so black a crime, and lack the moral courage to make expiation. . . . Oh ! do not let me feel I have been totally deceived in you !—prove to me that you are only a criminal, and not a coward,— that you are only weak, not utterly base. . . . But do not flatter yourself with the belief that you have anything to gain :—I am not asking a favour ; — I am simply demanding a right."

For one moment he remained stunned by her sentence as by a thunder-bolt surpassing all possible expectation : the next, he blanched to the whiteness of a dead man. She saw him pale,—as though shocked by the sudden vision of a great peril,—and watched him fearfully, wondering, doubting. Would he refuse to right himself in her eyes,—in God's eyes ?—must she despise him utterly ? But no !—his colour came back with a strong flush that made her heart leap.

—" I will do it," he made answer, in a voice of quiet resolve.

—" Then go ! " she said, with no change of tone.   Her face betrayed no gladness. . . . A moment more, and he had passed from her presence,—and she had not suffered herself to touch his vainly outstretched hand.


## XIII

And a year passed.

. . . She knew he had kept his word,— knew he had obeyed her in all things.   None of her secret fears had been realized.   He had totally changed his manner of life,—was living, self-exiled, in a distant city with his boy.   He had written often to her,—pleading passionate letters which were never answered. Was it that she doubted him still ?—or only that she doubted her own heart ?   He could not guess the truth.   He feared and hoped and waited ;—and season followed season.

Then one day she received a letter from him, bearing a postmark that startled her, because it revealed him so near,—a letter praying only to be allowed to see her, while passing through the suburb where she lived.

Another morning brought him the surprise of her reply. He kissed her name below the happy words : *" You may."*

## XIV

. . . " I have brought him to you," he said ;—" I thought you might wish it. . . . "

She did not seem to hear,—so intently was she looking at the boy, whose black soft eyes, beautiful as a fawn's, returned all timidly her clear, grey gaze. And from those shy dark orbs there seemed to look out upon her the soul of a dead woman, and a dead woman's pleading, and a dead woman's pain,—and the beauty and the frailty and the sorrow that had been,—until her own soul, luminous and pure and strong, made silent answer :—" Be never fearful, O thou poor lost one !—only by excess of love thy sin was : rest thou in thy peace ! " . . . And something of heaven's own light, like a softness of summer skies, made all divine her smile, as she knelt to put her arms about the boy and kiss him,—so that he wondered at the sweetness of her.

And the father, wondering more, hid his face as he sat there, and sobbing remained, until he knew her light hand upon his head, caressing him also, and heard her voice thrill to him with tenderness incomprehensible :—

—" Suffering is strength, my beloved !— suffering is knowledge, illumination, the flame that purifies ! Suffer and be strong. Never can you be happy : the evil you have wrought must always bring its pain. But that pain, dearest, I will help you to bear,— and the burden that is atonement I will aid you to endure ;—I will shield your weakness ;—I will love your boy. . . . "

For the first time their lips touched. . . . She had become again the Angel of his dream.

# A GHOST

# A GHOST

**P**ERHAPS the man who never wanders away from the place of his birth may pass all his life without knowing ghosts ; but the nomad is more than likely to make their acquaintance. I refer to the civilized nomad, whose wanderings are not prompted by hope of gain, nor determined by pleasure, but simply compelled by certain necessities of his being,— the man whose inner secret nature is totally at variance with the stable conditions of a society to which he belongs only by accident. However intellectually trained, he must always remain the slave of singular impulses which have no rational source, and which will often amaze him no less by their mastering power than by their continuous savage opposition to his every material interest. . . . These may, perhaps, be traced back to some ancestral habit,—be explained by self-evident hereditary tendencies. Or perhaps they may not,—in which event the victim can only surmise himself the *Imago* of some pre-existent larval aspiration—the full development of desires

63

long dormant in a chain of more limited lives. . . .

Assuredly the nomadic impulses differ in every member of the class,—take infinite variety from individual sensitiveness to environment : the line of least resistance for one being that of greatest resistance for another ;—no two courses of true nomadism can ever be wholly the same. Diversified of necessity both impulse and direction, even as human nature is diversified. Never since consciousness of time began were two beings born who possessed exactly the same quality of voice, the same precise degree of nervous impressibility, or,—in brief, the same combination of those viewless force-storing molecules which shape and poise themselves in sentient substance. Vain, therefore, all striving to particularize the curious psychology of such existences : at the very utmost it is possible only to describe such impulses and perceptions of nomadism as lie within the very small range of one's own observation. And whatever in these be strictly personal can have little interest or value except in so far as it holds something

64

in common with the great general experience of restless lives. To such experience may belong, I think, one ultimate result of all those irrational partings,—self-wreckings,—sudden isolations,—abrupt severances from all attachment, which form the history of the nomad . . . the knowledge that a strange silence is ever deepening and expanding about one's life, and that in that silence there are ghosts.

## II

. . . Oh ! the first vague charm, the first sunny illusion of some fair city,—when vistas of unknown streets all seem leading to the realization of a hope you dare not even whisper ;—when even the shadows look beautiful, and strange façades appear to smile good omen through light of gold ! And those first winning relations with men, while you are still a stranger, and only the better and the brighter side of their nature is turned to you ! . . . All is yet a delightful, luminous indefiniteness— sensation of streets and of men,—like some

beautifully tinted photograph slightly out of
focus. . . .

Then the slow solid sharpening of details
all about you,—thrusting through illusion
and dispelling it,—growing keener and harder
day by day, through long dull seasons, while
your feet learn to remember all asperities of
pavements, and your eyes all physiognomy
of buildings and of persons,—failures of
masonry,—furrowed lines of pain. Thereafter only the aching of monotony intolerable,
—and the hatred of sameness grown dismal,
—and dread of the merciless, inevitable,
daily and hourly repetition of things ;—while
those impulses of unrest, which are Nature's
urgings through that ancestral experience
which lives in each one of us,—outcries of
sea and peak and sky to man,—ever make
wilder appeal. . . . Strong friendships
may have been formed ; but there finally
comes a day when even these can give no
consolation for the pain of monotony,—and
you feel that in order to live you must
decide,—regardless of result,—to shake for
ever from your feet the familiar dust of that
place. . . .

66

## A GHOST

And, nevertheless, in the hour of departure you feel a pang. As train or steamer bears you away from the city and its myriad associations, the old illusive impression will quiver back about you for a moment,—not as if to mock the expectation of the past, but softly, touchingly, as if pleading to you to stay ; and such a sadness, such a tenderness may come to you, as one knows after reconciliation with a friend misapprehended and unjustly judged. . . . But you will never more see those streets,—except in dreams.

Through sleep only they will open again before you,—steeped in the illusive vagueness of the first long-past day,—peopled only by friends outreaching to you. Soundlessly you will tread those shadowy pavements many times,—to knock in thought, perhaps, at doors which the dead will open to you. . . . But with the passing of years all becomes dim—so dim that even asleep you know 'tis only a ghost-city, with streets going to nowhere. And finally whatever is left of it becomes confused and blended with cloudy memories of other cities,—one endless bewilderment of filmy architecture in which nothing is distinctly recognizable, though the whole gives the sensation of having been seen before . . . ever so long ago.

Meantime, in the course of wanderings more or less aimless, there has slowly grown upon you a suspicion of being haunted,—so frequently does a certain hazy presence intrude itself upon the visual memory. This, however, appears to gain rather than to lose in definiteness : with each return its visibility seems to increase. . . . And the suspicion that you may be haunted gradually develops into a certainty.

### III

You are haunted,—whether your way lie through the brown gloom of London winter, or the azure splendour of an equatorial day, —whether your steps be tracked in snows, or in the burning black sand of a tropic beach,—whether you rest beneath the swart shade of Northern pines, or under spidery umbrages of palm :—you are haunted ever and everywhere by a certain gentle presence.

There is nothing fearsome in this haunting
. . . the gentlest face . . . the kindliest
voice—oddly familiar and distinct, though
feeble as the hum of a bee. . . .

But it tantalizes,—this haunting,—like
those sudden surprises of sensation *within*
us, though seemingly not *of* us, which some
dreamers have sought to interpret as inherited
remembrances,—recollections of pre-exist-
ence. . . . Vainly you ask yourself :—
" Whose voice ?—whose face ? " It is neither
young nor old, the Face : it has a vapoury
indefinableness that leaves it a riddle ;—
its diaphaneity reveals no particular tint ;—
perhaps you may not even be quite sure
whether it has a beard. But its expression
is always gracious, passionless, smiling—like
the smiling of unknown friends in dreams,
with infinite indulgence for any folly, even a
dream-folly. . . . Except in that you cannot
permanently banish it, the presence offers no
positive resistance to your will : it accepts
each caprice with obedience ; it meets your
every whim with angelic patience. It is
never critical,—never makes plaint even by
a look,—never proves irksome : yet you

cannot ignore it, because of a certain queer power it possesses to make something stir and quiver in your heart,—like an old vague sweet regret,—something buried alive which will not die. . . . And so often does this happen that desire to solve the riddle becomes a pain,—that you finally find yourself making supplication to the Presence,—addressing to it questions which it will never answer directly, but only by a smile or by words having no relation to the asking,—words enigmatic, which make mysterious agitation in old forsaken fields of memory . . . even as a wind betimes, over wide wastes of marsh, sets all the grasses whispering about nothing. But you will question on, untiringly, through the nights and days of years :—

—" Who are you ?—what are you ?—what is this weird relation that you bear to me ? All you say to me I feel that I have heard before—but where ?—but when ? By what name am I to call you,—since you will answer to none that I remember ? Surely you do not live : yet I know the sleeping-places of all my dead,—and yours I do not know ! Neither are you any dream ;—for dreams distort and change ; and you, you are ever the same. Nor are you any hallucination ; for all my senses are still vivid and strong. . . . This only I know beyond doubt,—that you are of the Past : you belong to memory—but to the memory of what dead suns ? . . . "

Then, some day or night, unexpectedly, there comes to you at last,—with a soft swift tingling shock as of fingers invisible,—the knowledge that the Face is not the memory of any one face, but a multiple image formed of the traits of many dear faces,—superimposed by remembrance, and interblended by affection into one ghostly personality,—infinitely sympathetic, phantasmally beautiful : a Composite of recollections ! And the Voice is the echo of no one voice, but the echoing of many voices, molten into a single utterance,—a single impossible tone,—thin through remoteness of time, but inexpressibly caressing.

## IV

Thou most gentle Composite!—thou nameless and exquisite Unreality, thrilled into semblance of being from out the sum of all lost sympathies!—thou Ghost of all dear vanished things . . . with thy vain appeal of eyes that looked for my coming,—and vague faint pleading of voices against oblivion,—and thin electric touch of buried hands, . . . must thou pass away for ever with my passing,—even as the Shadow that I cast, O thou Shadowing of Souls? . . .

I am not sure. . . . For there comes to me this dream,—that if aught in human life hold power to pass—like a swerved sunray through interstellar spaces,—into the infinite mystery . . . to send one sweet strong vibration through immemorial Time . . . might not some luminous future be peopled with such as thou? . . . And in so far as that which makes for us the subtlest charm of being can lend one choral note to the Symphony of the Unknowable Purpose,—in so much might there not endure also to greet thee, another Composite One,—embodying, indeed, the comeliness of many lives, yet keeping likewise some visible memory of all that may have been gracious in this thy friend . . . ?

# THE FIRST MUEZZIN

If all that worship Thee to-day
Should suddenly be swept away,
And not a Muezzin left to cry
Through the silence of the sky,—
" God is Great ! "—there still would be
Clouds of witnesses for Thee
On the land and in the sea. . . .
Aye ! and if these, too, were fled,
And the earth itself were dead,
Greater would remain on high ;—
For all the planets in the sky,—
Suns that burn till day has flown,
Stars that are with night restored,—
Are Thy dervishes, O Lord,
Wheeling round Thy golden Throne !

EDWIN ARNOLD

# THE FIRST MUEZZIN

THE Traveller slumbering for the first time within the walls of an Oriental city, and in the vicinity of a minaret, can scarcely fail to be impressed by the solemn beauty of the Mohammedan Call to Prayer. If he have worthily prepared himself, by the study of books and of languages, for the experience of Eastern travel, he will probably have learned by heart the words of the sacred summons, and will recognize their syllables in the sonorous chant of the Muezzin,—while the rose-coloured light of an Egyptian or Syrian dawn expands its flush to the stars. Four times more will he hear that voice ere morning again illuminates the east :—under the white blaze of noon ; at the sunset hour, when the west is fervid with incandescent gold and vermilion ; in the long after-glow of orange and emerald fires ; and, still later, when a million astral lamps have been lighted in the vast and violet dome of God's everlasting mosque. Perhaps the last time he may distinguish, in the termination of the chant, words new and mysterious to his ear ; and should he question his dragoman,—as did Gerard de Nerval [1]—regarding their meaning, he would doubtless obtain a similar interpretation :—" O ye that are about to sleep, commend your souls to Him who never sleeps ! " Sublime exhortation !—recalling the words of that Throne-verse which jewelsmiths of the Orient engrave upon agates and upon rubies, — " *Drowsiness cometh not to Him, nor sleep.*" And if the interpreter should know something of the hagiology of Islam, he might further relate that the first Muezzin, the first singer of the *Adzân*, was the sainted servant of Mahomet,—even that Bilâli-bin-Rabah whose tomb is yet pointed out to travellers at Damascus.

Now Bilâl was an African black, an Abyssinian,—famed for his fortitude as a confessor,

---

[1] La première fois que j'entendis la voix lente et sereine du muezzin, au coucher du soleil, je me sentis pris d'une indicible mélancolie.— " Qu'est-ce qu'il dit ? " demandai-je au drogman. — " La Allah ila Allah ! . . . Il n'y a d'autre Dieu que Dieu ! " — " Je connais cette formule ; mais ensuite ? " — " O vous qui allez dormir, recommandez vos âmes à Celui qui ne dort jamais ! " — *Voyage en Orient*, " Le Drogman Abdullah."

for his zeal in the faith of the Prophet, and for the marvellous melody of his voice, whose echoes have been caught up and prolonged and multiplied by all the muezzins of Islam, through the passing of more than twelve hundred years. Bilâl sang before the idea of the first minaret had been conceived,—before blind men were selected to chant the *Adzân*, lest from the great height of the muezzin towers others might gaze upon the level roofs of the city, and behold sights forbidden to Moslem eyes. To-day innumerable minarets point to heaven : even the oases of the Sahara have their muezzin towers,—sometimes built in ignorance of the plumb-line, and so contorted that they seem to writhe, —like those at Ouargla which Victor Largeau saw in 1877. And the words chanted by all the muezzins of the Moslem world,—whether from the barbaric brick structures which rise above " The Tombs of the Desert," or from the fairy minarets of the exquisite mosque at Agra,—are the words first sung by the mighty voice of Bilâl.

Even at the present day many special qualifications are required of him who would

sing the *Adzân* : he must be learned in the
Koran : his name must be without reproach ;
his voice must be clear, suave and sonorous, his diction precise and pure.   But in the
earlier ages of Islam, while the traditional
memory of Bilâl's voice was strong in the
minds of the faithful, extraordinary vocal
powers may have been required of those
appointed to the office of muezzin.   Moslih-
Eddin Sadi, the far-famed Persian poet,
relates in his *Gulistan* more than one singular
anecdote illustrating the ideas of his day in
regard to the selection of muezzins and Koran-
readers. . . .   " Some one, in the Mosque of
Sandjar,"—he tells us,—" used to make the
Call to Prayer with good intent, yet with
a voice repugnant to all that heard it.   And
the Chief of the mosque was a just emir,
whose every action was good.   Accordingly
he sought to avoid giving a wound to the
heart of that man.   He spake to him thus,
saying : ' O sir ! there are old muezzins
attached unto this temple, to each one of
whom is allotted a salary of five dinars, and
verily I will give thee ten dinars to betake
thyself to another place.'   The man agreed

thereunto and went his way. But after a certain time he returned to the emir, and said to him : ' O my lord ! truly thou hast done me an injustice by inducing me to leave this monastery for ten dinars ! At the place to which I went they have offered me twenty dinars to go elsewhere,—and I refuse ! ' Then the emir smiled and made answer : ' Take heed thou accept them not ; for they will surely agree to pay thee even so much as fifty dinars ! ' " [1] ˎ

Not less amusingly significant is the anecdote which follows in the same portion of the book,—anecdote which will be more fully appreciated, doubtless, when we state that the old Arabian manner of reading the Koran ranks perhaps first among all preserved styles of religious cantillation :—" A man who had a disagreeable voice was reading the Koran aloud. A sensible man, passing by, asked of the reader : ' What is thy salary ? ' He answered : ' Nothing.' Then demanded the other,—' Wherefore dost thou take so much pains ? ' The man responded : ' I read for the love of God.' Then said the

[1] Chap. IV, *Upon the Advantage of Silence.*

other : ' O, for the love of God, do not read ! ' "

Son of an Abyssinian slave-girl, Bilâl began life as a slave.

Little seems to be known of his earlier years.

He was very dark,—" with negro-features and bushy hair," Sir William Muir tells us, upon the authority of Arabian writers ; he was also very tall, and gaunt as a camel ;— not comely to look upon, but vigorous and sinewy. Among the slaves of Mecca the first preaching of Mahomet took deep effect :—to the hearts of those strangers and bondsmen in a strange land of bondage, the idea of a Universal Father must have been a balm of consolation. Bilâl would seem to have been the first convert of his race, inasmuch as the Prophet was wont to speak of him as " the first-fruits of Abyssinia." Perhaps the young slave had obtained from his dark mother such rude notions of that Christianity implanted in Abyssinia during the fourth century, as might have prepared his mind to accept the monotheism of Islam.

But when the period of persecution com-

menced, it was upon those converted slaves
that the wrath of the idolatrous Koreish fell
most heavily. Among the Arabs it had been,
from time immemorial, a chivalric duty to
protect one's own kindred at the risk even of
life ; and the shedding of Arab blood by Arab
hands in time of peace never failed to provoke
such reprisals as often entailed a long war of
vendetta. By reason of this salutary social
law, Mahomet and his free Arab converts
felt themselves comparatively secure from
dangerous violence ; but the unprotected
slaves who had embraced the new faith were
cruelly beaten, often menaced with death,
and tortured by naked exposure to the
blistering sun. Under such suffering, to
which the torments of hunger and thirst were
superadded,—the temptations of cool water
and palatable food and shady rest proved
too much for the courage of the victims :
one by one they uttered, with their lips at
least, the prescribed malediction upon their
Prophet, and the idolatrous oath by Lat
and Ozza. Afterwards, many of them wept
bitterly for their recantation. But Mahomet
gave ample consolation to the poor renegades ;

and for their sake that special exemption for reluctant apostasy was provided in the Koran : —" *Whosoever denieth GOD after that he hath believed,*—EXCEPTING HIM WHO IS FORCIBLY COMPELLED THERETO, HIS HEART REMAINING STEADFAST IN THE FAITH—*on such resteth the wrath of God.*" [1]

Bilâl alone never apostatized : the agony of blows, the fiery pains of thirst, the long exposure to the sun upon the scorching gravel of the Valley of Mecca,—all failed to bend his iron will ; and to the demands of his persecutors he invariably answered,— *Ahad ! Ahad :* " One, one only God ! " This episode of his confessorship has been chosen by the poet Farid Uddin Attar as the text of a pious admonition contained in the superb invocation of the Mantic Uttair :— " Bilâl received upon his feeble body many blows with clubs of wood and thongs of leather : his blood flowed in abundance beneath the strokes,—yet never did he cease to cry out, ' God is one,—God is the only God ! ' "

It happened one day, while the poor

[1] Sura XVI, 108.

84

Abyssinian was being thus tormented, that a small, lithe, slightly built man, with handsome aquiline features and a singularly high forehead, suddenly appeared among the spectators of Bilâl's fortitude and suffering. This slender little man was the merchant Abdallah, son of Othman Abu Cahâfa,—but better known to students of Moslem history as Abu Bekr, famous as the bosom friend of the Prophet, his comrade in the Flight, and his companion in that famous cavern over whose entrance fond tradition avers that spiders wove a miraculous veil of webs to hide the fugitives,—Abu Bekr, also called *Al Siddick*, " the True," " father of the virgin," —father of Mahomet's future wife Ayesha, and destined to succeed him in the Khalifate. Already he had expended the greater part of a fortune of forty thousand dirhems in purchasing the freedom of slaves persecuted because of their conversion to Islam. These were mostly women or weaklings. " O my son ! " Abu Cahâfa was wont to say to him, —" I see that thou freest weak women ; but if thou wert to free strong men, they would stand by thee, and repel harm from thee."

" Nay, father ! " would Abu Bekr reply ;—
" I desire only those things which are of
God ! " And the Traditionists record that
by reason of this pious squandering of his
wealth, Al Siddick at last found himself
reduced to wear a coarse garment of goat's
hair, " pinned together at his breast with a
wooden skewer."

Abu Bekr did not long remain a silent
witness of Bilâl's resolution : he negotiated
upon the spot for the purchase of the slave,
and succeeded in obtaining him from his
owners—" Umayyah-b-Khàlàf and Ubayy-b-
Khàlàf "—for a cloak and ten pieces of
money. Little did any of the spectators of
that bargaining imagine the day would ever
come when Umayyah and his son might
vainly beg mercy from the slave to whom
they had shown no mercy. Ten years later,
after the furious battle of Bedr, it was Bilâl's
turn ; his keen eye singled out his former
owners from among the multitude of
Koreishite prisoners ; and it was his grim
satisfaction to have them slain before his face
—for the faith of Islam did not enjoin the
returning of good for evil.

86

## THE FIRST MUEZZIN

Now Bilâl was the first really valuable slave redeemed by Abu Bekr, who immediately after the purchase had set him free, ' for the love of God.' Bilâl was a powerful man; the feebleness spoken of by the Persian poet must only be understood as referring to the weakness of human nature by contrast with spiritual strength. Calumniators were not slow to declare that the Abyssinian had been bought free for purely selfish motives; a report apt to find credence in a community where the devout merchant had long been known as a shrewd speculator and a hard bargainer. Mahomet wrathfully rebuked this malicious gossip; and it is traditional that his reproof is embodied in the Ninetieth-and-second Sura of the Koran, entitled THE NIGHT,—comprising that part of its text from the opening line, *" By the Night when it covereth,"* to the close of the words, *" Verily, your endeavour is different ! "* . . .

Thus it happened that Bilâl obtained his manumission, to become the devoted servant of Mahomet, and to perform a great part in the expanding history of Islam. There is a legend that, after the Flight of the Prophet, he and others of the faithful temporarily remaining in Mecca, were again persecuted by the Koreish ; but this account is totally discredited by the best modern authorities upon the history of Mohammedanism. We next hear of Bilâl at Medina, in the character of The First Muezzin.


## II

During the infancy of Mohammedanism, when the faithful ones dwelt in the immediate vicinity of their prophet's home, the *Adzân* was unknown :—the simpler cry : *To public prayer !* being easily heard by all. It was not until after the building of the first mosque at Medina, and after Mahomet had changed the *Kibla*,—or the direction toward which the worshippers turned their faces—from Jerusalem to Mecca and its Kaaba, that the *Adzân* was established. But Jerusalem retains a large place in the Moslem legend and remains dear to Moslem faith ;— for hath it not been recorded in the Traditions that among the greater signs of the

Last Hour, shall be the coming of "Jesus the son of Mary" to Jerusalem even at the moment of morning prayer, when the Mosque of Omar will be lighted by the shining of His face, and He shall take the place of the awe-stricken Imam, and shall confound all those that call themselves Christians by uttering in mighty tones the great confession of Islam :—*Aschaduan na Mohammed rasoul Allah !*

The idea of the *Adzân* was obtained in a most singular way. After the building of that Mosque of Mahomet, which, despite the humbleness of its material, really formed the model for Saracenic architecture, it soon became evident that the old manner of summoning the congregation to worship was unsuited to the new conditions, and utterly devoid of that solemnity which ought to characterize all public performance of religious duty. At first the Prophet bethought him to have a trumpet made ; but having removed the *Kibla* from Jerusalem he could ill persuade himself to adopt an instrument used by the Jews in certain ceremonial observances. Then he thought of having a bell rung at certain regular hours ; but there was no one in Medina capable of making such a bell as he desired, and he had almost fixed his choice upon a wooden gong, when it came to pass that a certain citizen of Medina dreamed a strange dream.

It seemed to him that he beheld, passing through the moonlit street before his dwelling, a stranger uncommonly tall, clad in green raiment, and carrying in his hand a large and beautiful bell. And it seemed to the sleeper also, that, having approached the tall stranger, he asked : " Wilt thou sell me thy bell ? "—and that the tall man smilingly returned : " Tell me for what purpose thou seekest to buy it." " Verily," answered the dreamer in his dream,—" it is for our Lord Mahomet that I wish to obtain it, that he may therewith summon the faithful to prayer."

" Nay ! " said the stranger, seeming to grow taller as he spake,—" I will teach thee a better way than that ! Let a crier cry aloud, even thus. . . . " And in a voice so deep, so wonderful,—so superhumanly sonorous, so supernaturally sweet that a

90

great and holy fear came upon the listener, he chanted the *Adzân* of Islam,—even as it is chanted to-day, from the western coast of Africa to the eastern boundary of Hindostan:

> " *God is Great !*
> *God is Great !*
>
> *I bear witness there is no other God but God !*
> *I bear witness that Mahomet is the Prophet of God !*
>
> *Come unto Prayer !*
> *Come unto Salvation !*
> *God is Great !*
> *There is no other God but God !* "

. . . Awakening with the vibrant melody of that marvellous voice still in his ears, the good Moslem hastened to the Prophet with the story of his dream. Mahomet received him as one bearing a revelation from heaven ; and, remembering the uncommon vocal powers of his devoted Bilâl, bade the Abyssinian to sound the Call to Prayer, even as the words thereof had been revealed to the dreamer. It was yet deep night : ere dawn the First Muezzin had learned the duties of his new office, and at the earliest blush of day, the slumberers of Medina were aroused by the far-echoing and magnificent voice of the Abyssinian, chanting the *Adzân* from the summit of a lofty dwelling hard by the Mosque. . . . Does not the opening chapter in the history of the graceful Minaret—that architectural feature to which, above all others, the picturesqueness of Moslem cities is most largely due,—rightly begin with Bilâl's ascent to the starlit housetop in Medina, twelve hundred years ago?

And during all those centuries Islam has known no day in which the cry of the Muezzin has not gone up to God. Still the chanting of the *Adzân* times the passing of the hours for the populations of innumerable cities;[1] and it is among the Traditions that it shall also signal the approach of the last hour, the end of time,—when the last Imam Mahdi, the Antichrist of Moslem belief, shall announce his coming by singing the Call in

---

[1] It is rarely indeed that such an irregularity occurs as might have been suggested in the beautiful lines of Sadi :

" The Muezzin has lifted up his voice before the time : he knoweth not how much of the night is passed ! . . . Ask thou of mine eyes how long the night,—for sleep hath not visited mine eyelids even for one brief moment." —*Gulistan.*

so mighty a voice that the sound will roll around the world.

The summons to prayer has ever been obeyed with a scrupulous punctuality that evokes the surprise and admiration of travellers ; and this well-known Moslem fidelity to religious duty has, more than once in the history of Islam, been cruelly taken advantage of. It was at Nishapoor,—the city beloved of the *Perfumer of Souls*, that Attâr by whom Bilâl has been sung of in " The Language of Birds," that the *Adzân* was perhaps first chanted for a treacherous end. During the eighth year of the seventh century, the city was utterly destroyed by the hordes of Genghis Khan. In their rôle of exterminators the Tartars ever observed one practice unparalleled for sinister cruelty and cunning. This was, after having withdrawn from a wasted place, to suddenly return thither a few days later, so as to surprise any survivors who might have chanced to escape the fury of fire and sword, or such as might have returned to search for valued objects among the smouldering ruins. Returning thus to Nishapoor the Mongol leader caused the *Adzân* to be sounded; and by this brutal device it is said that many were lured from their secure refuges to slaughter. Well might a Persian historian say of those hordes : *"Their aim was the destruction of the human race and the ruin of the world, not the desire of dominion or of plunder."*

## III

In the luminous atmosphere of tradition, the voice of Bilâl vibrates for us like the voice of the Stranger in Green Raiment, superhumanly, paradisaically. After the lapse of so many hundred years it were difficult indeed to determine the precise character of the African's voice, or to particularize the indubitable merits of his chant. But if any rational inference whatever may be drawn from the highly florid evidence of the many traditions concerning him, we have a right to suppose that Bilâl's voice was a baritone of extraordinary range and volume, in strong contrast to the shrill and effeminate Arabian tenor. There is reason to doubt whether any of the singers famous in the annals of the pre-Islamic age, or " period of Ignorance "—Djâhéliâh—belonged to that race so effectively characterized by a French traveller as *un peuple criard*. As M. le Docteur Perron tells us in that delicious book *Les Femmes arabes* (published at Algiers in 1858), most of them were slaves; and nearly all the slaves held by the Arabs before the advent of Mahomet were Abyssinians or negroes. It is quite probable that those especially celebrated female singers, Youmad and Youad,—surnamed the *Djerradah Ad*, or Crickets of the Adides, and some of whose compositions are still extant,—were Abyssinian girls. They were owned by an Arab of the Beni Ad,—Abdallah, son of Djoudan,—concerning whom various beautiful traditions have been preserved. In almost all periods of Arabian history, mestizos, black freedmen, or the children of African slaves, found occasion to distinguish themselves as poets, artists or musicians. One of those swarthy singers, whom the Arabs termed by reason of their colour, "The Ravens," occupied so high a place that his songs are classed with the best productions of the best era

of Arabian poetry, and one of the immortal
mohallakats, or "Suspended Poems," bears
his name : Antarah.   Khoufaf, the warrior-
poet and cousin of the famous Khaysa—(one
of the greatest female singers of the desert)—
was a quadroon. Chanfara, another 'Raven,'—
a poet of no little merit,—singly declared war
against the whole tribe of the Benou-Abs who
had killed his father-in-law for no other
reason than that he dared to bestow his
daughter's hand upon the son of a slave.
Chanfara swore to kill a hundred men of
the tribe ;—ninety-nine fell beneath his hand,
before he was hunted down and slaughtered
like a wild beast ;—long afterward, one of
the Benou-Abs, trampling upon the bleaching
skull of the poet, lacerated his naked foot and
died of the wound, so that the oath of Chanfara
did not fail of accomplishment.   Mahomet
used often to regret that he had not lived
in the time of Antarah,—less, probably,
because he admired the poetry of the half-
breed nomad, than because he recognized
the value to his own cause of such a warrior-
singer, who could have rallied all the freedmen of the desert about the standard of a

Prophet who preached equality. The spirit of Islam gradually suppressed the beautiful poetry of the desert,—"warmly-coloured as the nature of that region, ardent as its sands, burning as its sun"; but although the 'Ravens' no longer composed mohallakats, they continued to sing. No small number of the celebrated musicians who flourished during the first three centuries of Islam[1] were half-breeds or blacks. Said-ibn-Mousadjih, whose goods were confiscated by order of the Caliph Abd-el-Mélik on the ground that by the charm of his singing he had excited the sons of the aristocracy to ruin themselves in giving him presents, was a negro of Mecca,[2] Abou Mahdjan Nossayb, son of the negro poet Rebah, was honoured by many governors and caliphs from the day of Abd-el-Mélik to the time

[1] See Caussin de Perceval :—*Notices anecdotiques sur les principaux musiciens arabes.*

[2] Said, however, went to Damascus, obtained an audience of the Caliph, and in lieu of pleading his case in words, sang one of his best compositions. On hearing him the Caliph restored the confiscated property, loaded the singer with gifts, and even declared he could excuse those who ruined themselves for the pleasure of hearing so mighty a singer.

of Hisham ;—Yezid II one day filled his
mouth with fine pearls. Abou Abbâd
Mabèd, prince of singers in his day, charmed
three Caliphs in succession. Yezid fainted
with delight at hearing the negro sing ;—
the succeeding Caliph once made him a gift
of 12,000 pieces of gold :—and Walid II,
in whose palace he died, led the funeral
*cortège* accompanied by his royal brother,
both attired in robes of mourning. The
singer Sallamah el-Zarka,—" the Brunette,"
—who received for a single kiss two pearls
worth 40,000 drachmas, was probably a
quadroon girl. Sallamah, or Sellamat-el-
Cass, of Medina, and Habbaba, her companion, were pretty half-breeds of Medina.
The story of Caliph Yezid's love for the
latter, and his death for grief at her loss, is one
of the most touching narratives in Arabian
history. Ample proof that the voices of
black slaves and their method of singing
possessed a peculiar charm for their Moslem
masters may be found in the works of most
celebrated Arabian and even Persian authors.
Ismail ibn-Djami of Mecca,—the greatest
singer of the golden Age of Islam,—once

paid a negress four dirhems to teach him a curious air that he heard her sing while carrying a water-jar upon her head. Afterward he sang the same air for Haroun el-Raschid, who declared he had never heard anything so original before, and paid the artist 4,000 pieces of gold as a reward,— together with a house luxuriously furnished, two men-servants and two pretty girl-slaves. Sadi the Persian poet has related sundry instances which show that negro-singers were still highly prized at a later day. The following anecdote is told in that portion of his *Gulistan* entitled " On the Manners of Dervishes " ;—and the poet relates it as a personal experience :

. . . " Once, voyaging to Hedjaz, a band of sensible youths were my friendly companions. Sometimes they murmured to themselves, and repeated certain mystic verses. And there was one with us, a Devotee, who disapproved the conduct of Dervishes, having indeed no knowledge of their suffering. Now when we had arrived at the Palmtree of the children of Helial, a young negro-boy came forth from an Arab encampment, and lifted up such a voice as might even have called down the birds of heaven. And I saw the camel of the Devotee become excited ; it cast its rider to the ground, and took its way to the desert. ' O Sheikh ! ' I cried, ' the voice of that child hath made impression even upon an animal, and yet hath made no impression upon thee.' "

It has been a custom among the Arabs, from prehistoric times, to encourage camels on the march by the chanting of verses ; and Gentius, commenting upon this fact in his quaint Latin translation of the *Gulistan* (Amsterdam, 1654), relates a still more extraordinary anecdote :

. . . " An author of much weight recounts that he himself, while travelling in the Arabian deserts, was once received at a house whose proprietor had just lost all his camels, —and that a little negro-slave came to him, and prayed him, saying : ' O traveller, thou wilt not displease my master by interceding with him for the pardon of my fault.' When they were at table, therefore, the traveller said : ' I will not partake of any nourishment until thou shalt have pardoned this slave his offence.' Then the master said: ' This slave is a rascal; he hath lost all my riches and reduced me to desperate straits . . . this slave is gifted with a most sweet voice; and having made him conductor of my camels, he so excited them to exertion by the charm of his singing that in one day they made a three days' journey; but upon being relieved of their loads at the end of the voyage, they all died. Nevertheless, in consideration of the hospitality I have accorded thee, I will remit the punishment which the slave deserves.' "

Another proof of the high esteem which singers proficient in this sort of chanting enjoyed in the Orient is afforded by an anecdote concerning the Caliph Al-Mansour, quoted in Jalal'uddin's history :—" Salem, the camel-driver, once drove Al-Mansour's camel, singing to it; and Al-Mansour was so excited with delight that he nearly fell from the animal, and he rewarded him with half a dirhem. The man said: ' I drove Hisham; and he rewarded me with ten thousand.' " . . .

It is beyond doubt, therefore, that during

the pre-Islamic era and for more than a century afterward, the musicians of the Arabians were chiefly slaves and generally half-breeds or blacks;[1] that these dark slaves often possessed phenomenal voices, and rose to high distinction by their skill in musical improvisation. We have no just reason to doubt that Bilâl may have been a really wonderful singer, and that the traditions regarding his vocal pre-eminence may have been founded upon fact. It remains to be considered whether he really established the method of chanting still followed by muezzins ; and whether he improvised the first *Adzân* music, or simply sang according to the teaching of his master Mahomet.

First of all, it must be remembered that notwithstanding their musical sensibility, music among the ancient Arabs scarcely rose above the grade of vocal improvisation,— sometimes resembling the modern Corsican *voceri*,—more generally being a sort of psalmody, " variegated and embroidered " according to the caprice of the singer and the effect he desired to produce,—the utter-

[1] See *Femmes arabes*, p. 467.

ance of each word being accompanied with an infinity of vocal flourishes, floritures, trills, modulations, so that to chant a cantilene of only three stanzas sometimes required as many hours of artistic exertion. This tendency survives among modern Arabs —" What traveller in Egypt," asks Perron, " has not heard these two words sung over and over again for half an hour at a time, or even more,—*La leîly* ?—O my Night ? " It is possible, nevertheless, that even in the time of Mahomet three distinct varieties of melody were recognized by Arabian musicians :

First,—that which was called *Straight :* a solemn or heroic style, suitable either for the chants of warriors or the songs of cameleers ;—

Second,—That which was called *Modulated* or *Composite,* consisting of very many different movements or effects of voice and tones ;—

Third,—That which was known as *The Light* or *Quick*—" affecting and stirring hearts, moving and troubling even serious minds."

As a slave, and therefore at times, no doubt, a conductor of camels, Bilâl may have been accustomed to chant in the measure called *Straight*; but as an African it is likely that the natural musical feeling of his race may have found utterance at other hours in melody of a less severe description,—such as the Arabs would have classed as *Modulated*. He should accordingly have been well able to improvise the melody of the *Adzân*, nor is it unreasonable to suppose that he did. Music heard in dreams is much less easily retained in the memory than are other incidents of slumber; the reader is doubtless familiar with the story of Tartini's *Trille del Diavolo*. It is hard to believe that the melody of the *Adzân* as chanted by the stranger in Green Raiment could have been so perfectly memorized by the dreamer as to be communicated to another person. On the other hand, it is not at all incredible that Bilâl, upon being taught the words, sang them in his own wild African way, and that Mahomet approved the melody,—just as he is known to have approved Bilâl's subsequent addition to the revealed *Adzân* of the words " *Prayer is better than sleep.*" Mahomet would have been likely to approve any improvisation ; for so highly did he esteem the Abyssinian that he was wont to ask his advice in matters of the greatest importance, and that although two other muezzins were subsequently appointed, they were never permitted to exercise their calling when it was possible for Bilâl to perform that duty. On the whole we have good reason to believe that the melody of the Call to Prayer was really improvised by Bilâl and that he chanted it with those singularities of modulation and weirdness of feeling still characteristic of African melody.

## IV

During the lifetime of the Prophet, Bilâl continued to be his constant attendant. Immediately after chanting the Call to Prayer, Bilâl would always arouse Mahomet with a pious ejaculation; and when the congregation had assembled within the Mosque, all eyes were fixed upon the African who stood in the front row, and whose genuflexions and prostrations were studiously imitated by the rest. It is still the duty of the muezzin to mingle his chant with that of the officiating Imam, to whom he occupies such a relation as that of the Christian deacon to the priest or minister. But as Islam grew in power, Bilâl's position greatly increased in importance, and far weightier duties were assigned to him :—in addition to his stewardship of Mahomet's household, he held the office of treasurer of the Prophet, receiving and keeping in trust all the revenues of the khalifate. When Mahomet made his triumphal entry into Mecca, it was Bilâl who received the keys of the Kaaba ; and it was Bilâl who first chanted the *Adzân* from the summit of that now world-famous temple. It was Bilâl who summoned Medina to prayer, when the princes came from the far-off land of Hadramaut "out of desire to embrace Islam." It was Bilâl who chanted the *Adzân* when the cavaliers of Islam camped in the desert to prepare for battle with the idolaters. Some sinister traditions of his savage zeal after the battles of Bedr and Kheibar reveal an unrelenting hatred to the enemies of his benefactor ; but these passages of his life need not be here detailed. It is more pleasant to remember that when Mahomet made his last pilgrimage to Mecca, the faithful black walked at his side to shade him with a rude screen from the noonday sun. Perhaps during that sultry journey over the glaring sand of the Holy Valley, Bilâl might have found himself treading the very spot where he and his fellow-slaves had once been tortured by the Koreish. . . .

But after the death of Mahomet other muezzins summoned the faithful of Medina to prayer. The wonderful voice was hushed ; for Bilâl made known his resolve never to sing the *Adzân* again. How long after the accession of Abu Bekr, Bilâl remained in the City of the Prophet is uncertain; but we know that he was more highly honoured by the faithful than ever before, and that he possessed influence enough to obtain a free-born Arab wife for his black brother—a remarkable condescension upon the part of a race whose noblest tribes are still distinguished by the surname *El H'rar*, or, " The Thoroughbreds." Even after the death of

Abu Bekr, Bilâl seemed to have exercised various important functions. When the austerely just Omar resolved to disgrace and supersede the " Sword of God," it was Bilâl who removed Khaled's helmet, and bound the warrior's hands before the assembly in the Mosque of Hims, exclaiming in his puissant voice : " Thus and thus the Commander of the Faithful hath said." . . . But after this episode we hear little of Bilâl until the visit of Omar to Syria. Thither the old man had followed the army ; and, having been granted land near Damascus, had retired altogether from public life.

Most of the Companions were dead ; Abu Bekr and Khaled had followed their Prophet to Paradise, together with a great host of those who had fought the first battles of Islam ; and the new generation was not like unto the old. The primitive and praiseworthy simplicity of the Bedouin tribes had almost disappeared from Arab life ;—strange Asiatic luxuries were being bought and sold in the cities of the desert ;—and the riches of Persia poured into Medina like a veritable inundation of gold, until Omar lifted up his voice and wept, saying—"Verily I foresee that the riches which the Lord hath bestowed upon us will become a spring of worldliness and envy, and in the end, a calamity unto my people!" The faith Bilâl had suffered for, the faith that had so long been unable to extend itself beyond the secluded quarter Abu Talib, had now imposed its supreme law upon Arabia, Syria, Palestine, Persia; and ere the venerable muezzin should for the last time commend his soul to Him Who never sleeps, the lands of Africa were to be added to the conquests of Islam; and the Call to Prayer was soon to be obeyed by nations of worshippers, from the confines of India even to the Atlantic shore. Already horsemen of the Arabian deserts had appeared before the gates of Cabul; and a son of Bilâl might have lived to see the Empire of the Prophet's successors extending over the greater portion of the earth's temperate zone,—from east to west two hundred days' journey. How must the fervent faith of the old man have been strengthened by the vast spectacle of Moslem power even in the eighteenth year of the Hegira!

After the death of Mahomet Bilâl ceased to sing the *Adzân* ;—the voice that had summoned the Prophet of God to the house of prayer ought not, he piously fancied, to be heard after the departure of his master. Yet, in his Syrian home, how often must he not have been prayed to chant the words as he first chanted them from that starlit housetop in the Holy City, and how often compelled to deny the petitions of those who revered him as a saint and would perhaps have sacrificed all their goods to have heard him but once lift up his voice in musical prayer ! . . . But when Omar visited Damascus the chiefs of the people besought him that, as Commander of the Faithful, he should ask Bilâl to sing the Call in honour of the event ; and the old man consented to do so for the last time.

The religious enthusiasm of the youth of Islam in those early years of the faith almost knew no bounds ; and the announcement that Bilâl would sing the *Adzân* must have enkindled such pious delight, such feverish exaltation among the people of that rose-scented city as we could find no parallel for in Christian history save in the period of the Crusaders. To hear Bilâl must have seemed to many as sacred a privilege as to have heard the voice of the Prophet himself, —the proudest episode of a lifetime,—the one incident of all others to be related in long after-years to children and to grandchildren. Some there may have been whom the occasion inspired with feelings no loftier than curiosity ; but the large majority of those who thronged to listen in silent expectancy for the *Allah-hu-akbar*, must have experienced emotions too deep to be ever forgotten. The records of the event, at least, fully justify this belief ;—for when, after moments of tremulous waiting, the grand voice of the aged African rolled out amid the hush,—with the old beloved words, the old familiar tones still deep and clear,— Omar and all those about him wept aloud, and tears streamed down every warrior-face, and the last long notes of the chant were lost in a tempest of sobbing.

What student of musical history would not wish to know how Bilâl sang that last *Adzân* ? —or to hear the words chanted precisely as the first Muezzin chanted them ? Needless to say that wish is absolutely impossible to realize. Utterly ignorant of the art of preserving music by written characters, the early Arabian melodists trusted to memory alone for the conservation of favourite airs or methods of cantillation ; and we shall never be able to determine whether Bilâl's improvisation has or has not been wholly lost. Nothing is left us but the privilege of a theory. Still, the theory may afford some consolation to the musical romanticists. We have some good reason to believe that melodies may be preserved by memory alone through more than a thousand years ; —there is even some ground for the supposition that certain Hebrew melodies have been transmitted unchanged through generations from the days of Solomon even to our own. Conservatism of religious tradition and practice was never less potent among the Arabs than among the Hebrews ;—the melody of the first *Adzân* might have had as fair a chance of being preserved as the religious melodies of Israel. It is at least barely possible that in the modern *Adzân* chant,

some fragment of Bilâl's cantillation may be
retained,—all the more so inasmuch as the
words of the Call to Prayer have not been
changed. Egypt, above all countries,—
conquered by the Moslem armies while
Bilâl was yet alive,—Egypt, the Land of
Changelessness, might have retained the
traditional memory of the chant as first
chanted in the second decade of the Hegira,
by muezzins who had heard Bilâl. And it
would indeed be pleasant to believe that
Bilâl himself sang the *Adzân* somewhat as
Villoteau heard it sung in modern Egypt,
with syllables of the name of God wrought
into arabesques of tones and fragments of
tones—so strangely impressive to Occidental
ears :—

The singer heard by Villoteau sang more
artistically, more ornately, than that muezzin
whose chant has been preserved for us by
Lane, and may be found in his *Account of
the Modern Egyptians*. Moreover, as a music-
loving friend points out to me, the cadences
of the second part in Lane's version all end
on the second of the minor scale—

—instead of the tonic— —as is

natural,—thus giving an impression of a chant suspended, unfinished. One might prefer to believe that Bilâl sang after the manner of the singer heard by Villoteau,— with all those Saracenic floritures, those fractions of tones that seem so nearly allied to the weird melodies of African improvisation. And still there is a pathetic and beautiful solemnity in the other and simpler chant, whose singular cadences seem to hold a pious intimation of the suggestion of the duty of worship, eternally beginning, yet never terminating,—of the prayer that may indeed be suspended, yet never finished,— of the adoration that may pause but never end—not even when the last muezzin shall have uttered the last call to prayer, and the last mosque shall have closed its gates for ever, and the spider shall weave her ghostly tapestries unmolested, within the deserted sanctuary of the Kaaba.

# CHINA AND THE WESTERN WORLD

## A RETROSPECT AND A PROSPECT ❧ ❧ ❧

# CHINA AND THE WESTERN WORLD

WHILE crossing any of the great oceans by steamer, and watching the dance of the waves that lift and swing the vessel, you sometimes become conscious of under movements much larger than those of the visible swells,—motion of surgings too broad to be perceived from deck. Over these unseen billowings the ship advances by long ascents and descents. If you carefully watch the visible waves, you will find that each one repeats the same phenomenon upon a very small scale. The smooth flanks of every swell are being rapidly traversed by currents of little waves, or ripples, running up and down. This surface-rippling is complicated to such a degree that it can be accurately noted only by the help of instantaneous photography. But it is so interesting to watch that if you once begin to observe it, you will presently forget all about the dimension and power of the real wave, the huge underswell over which the foaming and the rippling play.

In the study of those great events which

117

are the surges of contemporaneous history, that which corresponds to the currents and counter currents on the wave surface is apt to occupy public attention much more than the deeper under motion. All the confusion of details and theories furnished by official reports, by local observation and feeling, by the enterprise of trained newspaper correspondents, may have special value for some future historian ; but, like the ripples and the foam on the flanks of a wave, it covers from ordinary view that mightier motion which really made the event. Surges which break thrones or wreck civilizations are seldom considered in themselves at the moment of their passing. The sociologist may divine ; but the average reader will overlook the profounder meaning of the movement, because his attention is occupied with surface aspects.

The foreign press-comments upon the war between Japan and China have furnished many illustrations of this tendency to study the ripples of an event. Probably no good history of that war—no history based upon familiarity with complete records, and upon a thorough knowledge of the social and political conditions of the Far East anterior to 1893—can be written for at least another fifty years. Even the causes of the war have not yet been made fully known ; we have only official declarations (which leave immense scope for imagination) and a host of conflicting theories. One theory is that Japan, feeling the necessity of opening her territories to foreign trade, and fearing that China might take advantage of the revision of the treaties to flood the country with Chinese emigrants, declared war for the purpose of being able to exclude China from the privileges to be accorded to Western nations. Another theory is that war was declared because ever since 1882, when Li-Hung-Chang presented his Emperor with a memorial about plans for the " invasion of Japan," China had been preparing for an attack upon her progressive neighbour. A third theory is that Japan declared war in order to divert national feeling into less dangerous channels than those along which it had begun to flow. A fourth is that the declaration of war was designed to strengthen the hands of certain statesmen by creating a military revival. A fifth is that Japan planned the conquest of China merely to display her own military force. And there have been multitudes of other theories, some of them astonishingly ingenious and incredible ; but it is safe to say that no single theory yet offered contains the truth. Nevertheless, it has been altogether on the strength of such theories that Japan's action in declaring war has been criticized ; and many of the criticisms have been characterized by extraordinary injustice.[1]

Now, the critics of Japanese motives and morals have been in the position of persons studying only the currents and cross-currents upon the surface of a swell. For the ideas of statesmen, the diplomacy of ministers, the vague rumours suffered to escape from cabinet councils, the official utterances, the official correspondence, the preparations, the

[1] Especially those made by a portion of the London Press. How little the real condition of Japan was known up to the time of the war may be inferred from the fact that a leading English journal declared ten thousand Chinese troops could easily conquer Japan *because of the absence of national feeling in the latter country !*

proclamations,—all were but the superficial manifestations of the fact. The fact itself was that the vast tidal wave of Occidental civilization, rolling round the world, had lifted Japan and hurled her against China, with the result that the Chinese Empire is now a hopeless wreck. The deep, irresistible, underlying forces that set the war in motion were from the Occident; and this unquestionable fact once recognized, all criticisms of Japan from the moral standpoint become absurdly hypocritical. Another indubitable fact worth considering is that only by doing what no Western Power would have liked to attempt single-handed has Japan obtained the recognition of her rights and of her place among nations. She tore away that military scarecrow of Western manufacture which China had purchased at so great a cost, and exposed the enormous impotence which it had so long shielded.

## II

The spectacle of the power of Japan and the helplessness of China startled the Western world like the discovery of a danger. It was evident that the Japan of 1894 could execute without difficulty the famous menace uttered by Hideyoshi in the fourteenth century : " *I will assemble a mighty host, and, invading the country of the great Ming, I will fill with the hoar frost from my sword, the whole sky over the four hundred provinces.*" The idea of a China dominated by Japan at once presented itself to English journalists. It would be quite possible, they declared, for Japan to annex China, since the subjugation of the country would require little more than the overthrow of an effete dynasty and the suppression of a few feeble revolts. Thus China had been conquered by a Tartar tribe ; she could be subdued much more quickly by the perfectly disciplined armies of Japan. The people would soon submit to any rulers able to enforce law and order, while not interfering too much in matters of ancient custom and belief. Understanding the Chinese better than any Aryan conquerors could do, the Japanese would be able to make China the most formidable of military empires ; and they might even undertake to realize the ancient Japanese prediction that the Sun's Succession was destined to rule the earth. On this subject the *St James's Gazette* was particularly eloquent ; and a few of its observations are worth quoting, as showing the fancies excited in some English minds by the first news of the Japanese triumphs :—

" The Japanese dynasty would make no startling changes ; China would still be China, but it would be ' Japanned China.' An army and a navy, an organization by land and sea, would grow up under the hand of the Mikado. In ten or fifteen years' time a Chino-Japanese government would have an army of two millions of men armed with European weapons. In twenty-five years the available force might be five times as great, and the first couple of millions could be mobilized as quickly, let us say, as the armies of Russia. If such a power chose to start on a career of conquest, what could resist ? Nothing at present in Asia, not even Russia, could stand against it, and it might knock at the door of Europe. The combined Western Powers might resist the first shock,—might overcome the first five millions of Chinese riflemen and Tartar cavalry ; but behind that would come other five millions, army after army, until Europe itself was exhausted and its resources drained. If this seems a wild dream, consider what a Japan-governed China would be. Think what the Chinese are ; think of their powers of silent endurance under suffering and cruelty ; think of their frugality ; think of their patient perseverance, their slow, dogged persistence, their recklessness of life. Fancy this people ruled by a nation of born organizers, who, half allied to them, would understand their temperament and their habits. The Oriental, with his power of retaining health in conditions under which no European could live, with his savage daring when roused, with his inborn cunning, lacks only the superior knowledge of civilization to be the equal of the European in warfare as well as in industry. In England

124

we do not realize that in a Japanese dynasty
such a civilization would exist : we have
not yet learned to look upon the Mikado as
a civilized monarch, as we look upon the
Czar. Yet such he is, undoubtedly. And
under him the dreams of the supremacy
of the yellow race in Europe, Asia, and even
Africa, to which Dr Pearson and others have
given expression, would be no longer mere
nightmares. Instead of speculating as to
whether England or Germany or Russia is
to be the next world's ruler, we might have
to learn that Japan was on its way to that
position."

The reference to Dr Pearson shows, as
we shall see hereafter, that his views had
not been carefully studied by the writer.
But the possibilities suggested by the *Gazette*
may be said to have really existed, pre-
supposing non-interference by Western
Powers. Interference was, of course, inevitable ; but the danger imagined from Japan
reappears in another form as a result of the
interference. China under a Russian domination would be quite as dangerous to the
Occident as under a Japanese domination.

Russia is probably a better military organizer than Japan, and would scarcely be more scrupulous in the exploitation of Chinese military resources. If the Japanese believe that their dynasty will yet hold universal sway, not less do Russians believe that the dominion of their Czar is to spread over the whole world. For the Western Powers to allow Russia to subjugate China would be even more dangerous than to suffer Japan to rule it. But while it would have been easy to prevent the annexation of China by Japan, it will not be easy to prevent the same thing from being done by Russia.

A host of unpleasant political problems have thus been brought into existence. What is to be done with China, now practically at the mercy of Russia ? Is her vast territory to be divided among several Western Powers, as Russia desires ? Is her empire to be repropped and maintained, like that of Turkey, so as to preserve peace ? Nobody can answer such questions just now. Nothing is even tolerably certain except that China must yield to Western pressure, and that she will be industrially exploited to the uttermost, sooner or later. Meanwhile, she remains a source of peril,—the possible cause of a tremendous conflict.

Momentous as all this may seem, the new political questions stirred up by the fall of China from her position as the greatest of Far-Eastern nations are really surface questions. The most serious problem created by the late war is much broader and deeper. No international war or any other possible happening is likely to prevent the domination of China by some form of Occidental civilization ; and when this becomes an accomplished fact we shall be face to face with the real danger of which Dr Pearson's book was the prediction. All future civilization may be affected by such domination ; and even the fate of the Western races may be decided by it. The great Chinese puzzle to come is neither political nor military ; it cannot be solved either by statecraft or by armies ; it can be decided only by the operation of natural laws, among which that of physiological economy will probably be the chief. But just as English critics of the late war ignored the real cause of that war,

127

the huge westward surge of forces that compelled it, so do they now ignore the fact that the same war has set in motion forces of another order which may change the whole future history of mankind.

## III

The Far-Eastern question of most importance was first offered for English sociological consideration in Dr Pearson's wonderful volume, *National Life and Character*, published about three years ago.[1] While reading a number of criticisms upon it, I was struck by the fact that a majority of the reviewers had failed to notice the most important portions of the argument. The rude shock given by the book to the Western pride of race, to the English sense of stability in especial, to that absolute self-confidence which constantly impels us to the extension

[1] By Macmillan & Co. in 1893. In the *Revue Bleue* and other French periodicals some phases of the question had been previously treated by able writers, but in so different a manner that the whole of Dr Pearson's work appears as a totally original presentation of the subject.

of territory, the creation of new colonies, the development of new resources reached by force, without any suspicion that all this aggrandizement may bring its own penalty, provoked a state of mind unfavourable to impartial reflection. The idea that the white races and their civilization might perish, in competition with a race and a civilization long regarded as semi-barbarous, needed in England some philosophical patience to examine. Abroad the conditions were otherwise. Far-seeing men, who had passed the better part of their lives in China, found nothing atrocious in Dr Pearson's book. It only expressed, with uncommon vigour and breadth of argument, ideas which their own long experience in the Far East had slowly forced upon them. But of such ideas, it was the one that most impressed the Englishman in China which least impressed the Englishman in London. A partial reason may have been that Dr Pearson's arguments in 1893 appeared to deal with contingencies incalculably remote. But what seemed extremely remote in 1893 has ceased to seem remote since the victories of Japan. The fate of China as an empire can scarcely now be called a matter of doubt, although the methods by which it is to be decided will continue to afford food for political speculation. China must pass under the domination of Western civilization ; and this simple fact will create the danger to which Dr Pearson called attention.

It is true that the author of *National Life and Character* did consider the possibility of a military awakening of China ; but he also expressed his belief that it was the least likely of events, and could hardly be brought about except through the prior conversion of all China to the warrior-creed of Islam. Recent events have proved the soundness of this belief ; for the war exposed a condition of official cowardice and corruption worse than had ever been imagined,—a condition which could not fail to paralyze any attempt to rouse the race out of lethargy. With the close of the campaign the world felt convinced that no military regeneration of China was possible under the present dynasty. Spasmodic attempts at revolution followed ; but some of these exhausted themselves in the

130

murder of a few foreign missionaries and in foolish attacks upon mission stations, with the usual consequences of Christian retaliation,—executions and big indemnities ; and other uprisings, even in the Mohammedan districts, have failed to accomplish anything beyond local disorder. Nothing like a general revolution now appears possible. Without it the reigning dynasty cannot be overthrown except by foreign power ; and under that dynasty there is not even the ghost of a chance for military reforms. Indeed, it is doubtful if the Western Powers would now permit China to make herself as strong as she was imagined to be only two years ago. In her present state she will have to obey those Powers. She will have to submit to their discipline within her own borders, but not to such discipline as would enable her to create formidable armies. Nevertheless, it is just that kind of discipline which she will have to learn that is most likely to make her dangerous. *The future danger from China will be industrial, and will begin with the time that she passes under Occidental domination.*

## IV

For the benefit of those who have not read his book, it may be well to reproduce some of Dr Pearson's opinions about this peril, and also to say a few words about the delusion, or superstition, which opposes them. This delusion is that all weaker peoples are destined to make way for the great colonizing white races, leaving the latter sole masters of the habitable world. This flattering belief is without any better foundation in fact than the extermination of some nomadic and some savage peoples of a very low order of capacity. Such extinctions have been comparatively recent, and for that reason undue importance may have been attached to them. Older history presents us with facts of a totally different character, with numerous instances of the subjugation of the civilized by the savage, and of the destruction of a civilization by barbarian force. It would also be well to remember that the most advanced of existing races is very far from being the highest race that has ever existed. One race, at least, has disappeared which was immensely superior, both physically and morally, to the English people of to-day. I quote from Francis Galton : " The average ability of the Athenian race was, on the lowest possible estimate, nearly two grades higher than our own,—that is, about as much as the ability of our race is above that of the African negro. This estimate, which may seem prodigious to some, is confirmed by the quick intelligence and high culture of the Athenian commonalty, before whom literary works were recited, and works of art exhibited, of a far more severe character than could possibly be appreciated by the average of our age,—the calibre of whose intellect is easily gauged by a glance at the contents of a railway bookstall. . . . If we could raise the average standard of our own race only *one* grade, what vast changes would be produced ! . . . The number of men of natural gifts equal to those of the eminent men of the present day would be increased tenfold [2433 to a million, instead of 233]." Mr Galton goes on to prove that, could we raise the average ability to the Athenian level, or *two* grades higher, the result would be that for every six men of extraordinary ability whom England can now produce, she would then produce thirteen hundred and fifty-five.[1] Perhaps so gifted a race will never again appear upon earth. Yet it has utterly disappeared. Probably the remark will be made that its disappearance was due chiefly, as Mr Galton seems to believe, to moral laxity. Well, the very title of Dr Pearson's book ought to have indicated to those who reviewed it superficially that he was considering the probable results of moral laxity upon modern civilization. One of our dangers is to be sought in the ever-increasing greed of pleasure and the decay of character. The mental and the moral capacities of the so-called higher races are showing, Dr Pearson believed, those signs of exhaustion which

[1] *Hereditary Genius,* " On the Comparative Worth of Different Races," pp. 329–332, edition of 1892. Concerning the physical development of the Greek race, I would recommend the reader to glance at Taine's extraordinary grouping of evidence bearing on the question, in his *Philosophie de l'Art* and in *L'Idéal dans l'Art.* Mr Mahaffy has written a book to prove the English boy superior to the Greek boy ; but his argument involves the denial of facts accepted by equally good authority.

would indicate that the maximum development of our civilization has almost been reached. The fact is certainly significant that the most naturally gifted of all European races, the French, is showing itself, like the Athenian race, relatively though not normally infertile. There are doubtless other causes for this, such as those considered by Mr Spencer ;[1] but the decay of character can scarcely be the least. For all Occidental civilization this will be one of the perils from within. The peril from without will be the industrial competition of the Far East.

Before we consider Dr Pearson's views, another remark may be offered about the exaggerated belief of the Western races in their own unparalleled superiority. Monstrous as may seem to some the fancy that a non-Christian Oriental race may be able to dominate Christendom in the future, we have to face the fact that a non-Christian and an Oriental people financially rule Western civilization to-day. The world's finances are practically in the hands of a

[1] *Principles of Biology*, vol. ii, chap. xii.

race persecuted by Christianity for thirteen centuries,—a race undoubtedly modified in the Occident by large interfusion of Western blood, but nevertheless markedly preserving its Oriental and unmistakable characteristics. And the recent anti-Semitic manifestations in Europe represent the modern acknowledgment of Aryan inability to cope with particular powers possessed by that race. I might even cite from a remarkable German study, published about ten years ago, and written to prove that whenever the percentage of Hebrews in a Gentile population begins to exceed a certain small figure, then " life becomes intolerable for the Gentiles." But I wish to call attention to general rather than to special superiority. The intellectual power of the Jew is by no means limited to business. The average of Jewish ability surpasses that of the so-termed Aryan in a far greater variety of directions than is commonly known. Out of 100,000 Western celebrities, the proportion of Jews to Europeans in philology, for example, is 123 to 13 ; in music, it is 71 to 11 ; in medicine, it is 49 to 31 ; in natural science, it is

25 to 22.[1] In departments of genius as diverse as those of chess-playing and acting, the Jewish superiority is also powerfully marked. It has been said that the Jewish capacity was developed by Christian persecution; but, not to mention the fact that such persecution selected its victims rather from the best than from the worst of a Jewish population, this explanation would place within comparatively recent times the evolution of mental powers which have distinguished the race from the most ancient times. Jewish capacity was rather the cause than the consequence of persecution. Ages before Christianity (as might be inferred even from Genesis and from Exodus, or from the book of Esther) the race had been hated and persecuted because of its capacity. That capacity was restrained by special legal disabilities in Rome. It provoked murder and pillage even under the tolerant rule of the Arabs in Spain;[2] and the attitude of Mohammedan

---

[1] I take the figures accepted by Lombroso. See his *Man of Genius.*

[2] For particulars of the rising against the Jews in Spain under the Arabs, see Dozy's *History.*

137

races toward the Jews in Africa and in Asia has been, on the whole, scarcely more tolerant than that of Christian nations.

So much for the fancied mental supremacy of the Western nations. The delusion that other races are providentially destined to disappear before the so-called Aryan, has been attacked by Dr Pearson with a vast array of systematized facts and observations, including the results of studies made by himself in many parts of the world. Although it is true that some races, unable to bear the discipline of our civilization, have already disappeared, or are quickly disappearing,—such as the Tasmanian and Australian aborigines, certain Maori peoples, and North American Indian tribes,—Dr Pearson has shown that these accomplished or threatened extinctions illustrate only the exceptions to the general rule of the effect of Western expansion upon alien races. Under our social system the condition of being able to live is to work hard, to work steadily, and to work intelligently. Those unable to do this either perish at once, or sink into the slough of vice and crime which underlies all our civilization, or else find themselves reduced to a condition of misery worse than any normal experiences of savage life. But there are many inferior races, both savage and semi-savage, which thrive under the discipline of the higher races, and so multiply after the introduction of Occidental order into their territory that their multiplication itself becomes an effective check upon the further growth of the dominating race. Thus the Kaffir has multiplied under British protection, and the Javanese under Dutch. Thus the populations of the Straits Settlements and of British India steadily increase. The history of the various English, French, and Dutch colonies yields wide evidence that many weaker races, far from vanishing before the white, greatly increase in number. Such increase necessarily sets a limit to white multiplication in those regions,—seeing that all labour needed can be supplied by natives at rates for which no white men would work, even supposing the climate were in all cases favourable to Europeans.

Climate, however, is another question in this relation. Climate also sets a limit—

probably a perpetual limit—to the expansion of the higher races. The tropics, apparently, can never become their habitat. In what has been termed the ' pyrogenic region ' the white races cannot maintain themselves without the aid of other races. Their domination now, as in the past, we find to depend upon constant supplies of fresh strength from a colder region, and their numbers have never increased beyond an insignificant figure. The West Indies, from which the white race is slowly but surely vanishing, furnish a strong example : the estates are passing into the hands of the former slave race. Tropical Africa may be held, but never can be peopled by Europeans. Left to themselves for a few generations, the English in Hindustan would vanish utterly, like those Greek conquerors who, after Alexander, ruled Indian kingdoms. The state of Spanish and Portuguese tropical colonies in both hemispheres tells eloquently the story of the limits set by Nature to white expansion.[1]

---

[1] Long before Dr Pearson, Herbert Spencer had noticed these limits. He had also observed, " With social organisms, as with individual organisms, the

In the temperate zone, where the Western races come into contact with races indubitably civilized, though in some respects less highly organized, the former can only temporarily gain ground, for the white races can be most effectually underlived by peoples of nearly equal intelligence in production and in commerce. The Occidentals may conquer and rule, but they have even less chance of multiplying at the expense of Chinese than of multiplying at the expense of Hindus. All the great Oriental races have proved themselves able to learn enough of the wisdom of the West to more than hold their own in matters of manufacture and trade. Under Occidental government a civilized Oriental race not only grows, but grows rich. In the matter of labour, whether common or skilled, the white artisan has no chance to compete with Orientals upon their own soil, or—except in the manufactures wholly depending upon the applied sciences

evolution of superior types does not entail the extinction of all inferior ones " (*Sociology*, vol. ii). But Mr Spencer has never given detailed attention to the special problems first studied in detail by the author of *National Life and Character.*

—upon any other soil. White labour has never been able to compete on equal terms with Oriental labour.

## V

Those confessions, which all European nations have made at various epochs of their history,—and which some have made in our own time,—of inability to cope with the Jewish people upon equal terms have other sociological meanings than such as might be implied by difference in average mental ability. They must also be considered as suggestive of the incapacity of societies not yet emerged from the militant stage to compete with a people essentially commercial from an epoch long anterior to the foundation of those societies. It is noteworthy that just in proportion as the militant form of society has changed toward the industrial, anti-Semitic feeling has diminished, whereas it is strengthened again by any reverse social tendency. The most essentially industrial nations, America and England, to-day give no exhibitions of anti-

Semitic feeling; but with the military expansion of other societies or the marked return to military forms we find the sentiment reviving. Russia, Germany, and even republican France have given manifestations of it; those of Russia proving absolutely medieval and ferocious.

Now, we must remember, while considering the question of future race competition in the Far East, that the evolution of Occidental civilization from the militant toward the industrial state is yet far from complete, as its propensities to aggression bear witness; while the Chinese, however much below our level in certain phases of development, are a people that reached the industrial type of society thousands of years ago.

In Dr Pearson's book it is plainly stated that the industrial competition of China would be incomparably more dangerous to Western civilization than that of any other nation, not only because of its multiformity, but also because it is a competition to which Nature has set no climatic limits. Thrifty and patient and cunning as Jews, the Chinese can accommodate themselves to any climate and to any environment. They can live in Java or in Siberia, in Borneo or in Thibet. Unlike the modern Jews, however, they are more to be feared in industry than in commerce ; for there is scarcely any form of manual skilled labour at which they are not capable of killing white competition. Their history in Australia has proved this fact. But in commerce also they are able to hold their own against the cleverest merchants of other races. They are adepts at combination, excellent financiers, shrewd and daring speculators. Though not yet rivals of Europeans in that class of production dependent upon the application of modern science to manufacture, they have given proof of ability to master that science whenever the study can profit them. They are learning thoroughly the commercial conditions of every country which they visit ; and though the history of their emigration began within recent times, they are already to be found in almost every part of the world. They have swarmed along the coasts of North and South America, and found their way to the West Indies. A big part of the East knows them. They do business in the cities of India ; they created Singapore. They have multiplied in the Malay peninsula, in Sumatra, in Hawaii, in numbers of islands. They are said to have provoked, by threatening the existence of Dutch rule in Java, the massacre in which nine thousand of their race perished. Both Australia and the United States have found it necessary to legislate against their immigration ; and the Chinese ability to supplant the Malay races in the Eastern tropics has produced astonishing results within the memory of men now living.

What America and Australia have been obliged to protect themselves from, all Europe may have cause to fear before the close of the next century. Once China has been penetrated by the forces of Western civilization, her population will begin to display new activities, and to expand in all possible directions. Chinese competition will have to be faced, probably, very much sooner than had been expected.

## VI

A very significant fact bearing upon this problem has been furnished by the influence of Occidental civilization in Japan.

Although the author who declared the Western type of society to be, in many respects, " one of the most horrible that has ever existed in the world's history " was certainly more than half right ; although it is true that we see " boundless luxury and self-indulgence at one end of the scale, and at the other a condition of life as cruel as that of a Roman slave, and more degraded than that of a South-Sea islander " ; although our civilization be one which opens the gate of fortune to aggressive cunning, and closes it as long as possible against the highest qualities of character and of intellect,—nevertheless that civilization enormously multiplies the chances for energy, for talent, for practical abilities of almost every description. While crushing and destroying in one direction, it opens a hundred ways for escape in another. Though the feeble, the stupid, and the vicious are brayed alive, the strong, the clever, and the self-controlled are not only aided, but are compelled to better themselves. The condition of success is not merely that effort shall be constant, but also that the force of the effort itself shall be constantly increased ; and those able to fulfil that condition without a mental or a physical break-down are tolerably certain to win at last what they wish,—perhaps even more than they wish. While the effort exacted is large, the return is, in the majority of normal cases, more than proportional. Life must be lived upon a bigger scale than in the past ; but the means so to live can be earned by the more vigorous. Although, by the law of antagonism between individuation and genesis, the higher races ought to be the less fertile races, other conditions being equal, they are not so, having been able to create for themselves conditions unknown in previous eras, and opportunities still undreamed of by races accustomed to simple natural living. Hence the phenomenon that a non-Aryan race, able and willing to adopt Western civilization, or even to submit contentedly to its discipline, will begin to multiply more rapidly under the new conditions, even while those conditions entail forms of suffering previously unknown. Up to a certain stage of development the opportunities of life will be increased even more than the difficulties ; for previous resources will be enlarged, and new ones found and developed, while countless means of conquering natural obstacles will be furnished by scientific knowledge to those capable of using them.

Penetrated by the influences of Western civilization, the population of Japan began almost simultaneously to expand. Within twenty-two years it has increased *more than twenty-five per cent*. In the year 1872 it was 33,110,825. In 1892 it was 41,388,313. It is now over 42,000,000. And this increase has been in despite of repeated epidemics, and great losses of life due to floods and earthquakes. Improved sanitation, enforcement of hygienic laws, attention given to drainage and to systems of water supply have certainly helped the increase, but could not alone explain it. The explanation is to be sought rather in the greatly widened oppor-

148

tunities of life furnished by the sudden development of the country. During the same period the increase in the total volume of the export and import trade has been 534 per cent. The total of customs duties has more than quadrupled. Wages are said to have risen 37 per cent.[1] Among facts showing agricultural development is the increase in the area of cultivated land. That of land under wheat and barley is put at 58·5 per cent., and of land under rice at 8·4. Improved methods of agriculture may help to account for the increase of rice production by 25·5 per cent. during the last fifteen years alone. In the same period of fifteen years, the increase in silk production has been 300·2 per cent., and in that of tea 240·3. In the year 1883 there were 84 manufactories using steam or hydraulic power. In the year 1893 there were 1163 ; in

[1] Probably at the open ports only. I take these figures from the Japan *Daily Mail*, which republished them from the *Kokuminno-Tomo*. I personally know, however, that in some provinces there has been yet practically no rise in wages worth mentioning. The cost of skilled labour in the open ports has increased greatly.

cotton-spinning the development has been enormous, — 1014 per cent. in a single decade.

I think that the myriad new opportunities to earn a little more than a good living which this immense expansion implies should suffice of themselves to account for that increase of population which is even now offering a new problem to the Japanese Government, and which has been only temporarily met by the acquisition of Formosa and the Pescadores, by the project for a Japanese Mexican colony, by the shipment of labourers to Hawaii and to other places, and by the overflow into Australia, where the Japanese labour question threatens to become as unpleasant as was the Chinese question in Dr Pearson's time. The whole meaning of this increase of population will best appear when I remind the reader that, in one sense of the term, the Japanese are by no means a fertile race. Large families are comparatively rare,—a family of nine or ten children being quite uncommon, and the birth of twins so rare as to be considered an anomaly. Nevertheless, the Japanese population has increased over 25 per cent., while that of England has increased only about 7 per cent. This, of course, is temporary, and a check must eventually come ; but the period of that check is apparently still far off.

Imagine, then, the consequence of a corresponding commercial and industrial development upon a Chinese population of four or five hundred millions,—probably more fertile than the Japanese, declared by the Japanese themselves superior in all the craft of commerce and the secrets of finance, matchless as mere mechanical workers, and capable of living and multiplying under conditions according to which the Japanese artisan would refuse to live ! Compel China to do what Japan has voluntarily done, and the increase of her population within one century will probably be a phenomenon without parallel in the past history of the world.

## VII

Here, however, there come up some doubts to be considered. *Can* China be forced to develop herself as Japan has done? And is not Western industrialism likely to be protected from Chinese competition by the irreducible character of Chinese conservatism? Japanese development has been voluntary, patriotic, eager, earnest, unselfish. But will not the Chinaman of the year 2000 resemble in all things the familiar Chinaman of to-day?

I must presume to express a conviction that the character of Chinese conservatism has never been fully understood in the West, and that it is just in the peculiar one-sidedness of that conservatism that the peril reveals itself. Japan has certainly been more thoroughly studied than China; yet even the character of Japan was so little understood two years ago that her defeat by China was predicted as a matter of course. Japan was imagined to be a sort of miniature of China, —probably because of superficial resemblances created by her adoption of Chinese civilization. It often occurs to me that the old Jesuit missionaries understood the difference of the races infinitely better than even our diplomats do to-day. When, after having studied the wonderful, quaint letters of these ecclesiastics, one reads the judgments uttered about the Far East by modern journalists, and the absurdly untruthful reports sent home by our English and American missionaries, it is difficult to believe that we have not actually retrograded, either in common honesty or in knowledge of the Orient. I tried to make plain in a former paper [1] that a characteristic of Japanese life was its fluidity; and also that this characteristic was not of yesterday. All the modern tales about the former rigidity of Japanese society —about the conservation of habits and customs unchanged through centuries—are mostly pure fiction. The assimilative genius of the race is the proof. Assimilative genius is not the characteristic of a people whose customs and habits have been conservatively fixed beyond the reach of change. "A mind that would grow," said Clifford, "must

[1] See *The Atlantic Monthly* for October 1895.

let no ideas become permanent except such as lead to action. Towards all others it must maintain an attitude of absolute receptivity,—admitting all, being modified by all, but permanently biased by none. To become crystallized, fixed, in opinion and mode of thought is to lose that great characteristic of life by which it is distinguished from inanimate nature,—the power of adapting itself to circumstances. This is true even of the race. . . . And if we consider that a race, *in proportion as it is plastic and capable of change,* may be considered as young and vigorous, . . . we shall see the immense importance of checking the growth of conventionalities." [1]  The relation between the essentially mobile and plastic character of Japanese society and that assimilative genius which could successively adopt and remodel for its own peculiar needs two utterly different forms of civilization should certainly be obvious. But according to the same sociological law expressed by Professor Clifford, the Chinese race would be doomed to

[1] *Lectures and Essays,* " Some Conditions of Mental Development."

154

disappear, or at least to shrink up into some narrow area—supposing it really incapable of modification. In Europe the generally received opinion about China seems to be that her conservatism is like the conservatism of the ancient Egyptians, and must eventually leave her people in a state of changeless subservience like that of the modern fellaheen. But is this opinion true?

Perhaps we should look in vain through the literature of any other equally civilized people for a record like that in the Li-Ki, which tells us that anciently, in China, persons " guilty of changing what had been definitely settled," and of using or making " strange garments, wonderful contrivances, and extraordinary implements," were put to death! But modern China is not to be judged by her ancient literature, but by her present life. Men who know China also know that Chinese conservatism does not extend to those activities which belong to trade, to industry, to commerce or speculation. It is a conservatism in beliefs, ethics, and customs, and has nothing to do with business. A conservatism of this sort may be a source of power ; it is not likely to be a source of weakness. Whether in Japan or in India, Canada or Australia, Cuba or Chili, Siberia or Burmah, the Chinaman remains a Chinaman. But while so remaining he knows how to utilize the modern inventions of industry, the modern facilities of communication, the new resources of commerce. He knows the value of cable codes ; he charters steamers, builds factories, manages banks, profits by the depreciation or the rise of exchange, makes 'corners,' organizes stock companies, hires steam or electricity to aid him in his manufacturing or speculating.[1] As a merchant his commercial integrity is recognized by the foreign merchants, of every nation, who deal with him. He keeps his costume and his creed, observes his national rules of propriety, maintains his peculiar cult

---

[1] At the time of the great silver depreciation a clever trick was reported from one of the Chinese open ports. Some Chinese forgers were able to put into circulation a considerable quantity of unlawful coin ; but when the coin was examined it proved to be true metal ! Nevertheless, a handsome profit must have been made, because of the temporary difference between the market price of silver and the value of the money.

at home; but the home may be a granite front in America, a bungalow in India, a bamboo hut in Sumatra, a brick cottage in New Zealand, a fire-proof two-story in Japan. He avails himself of the best he can afford abroad when the use of the best is connected with a commercial advantage; and when this is not the case he can put up with much worse than the worst. His conservatism never interferes with his business: it is a domestic matter, a personal matter, affecting only his intimate life, his private expenditure. His pleasures and even his vices—provided he be not a gambler—are comparatively inexpensive; and he clings to the simplicity of his ancestral habits even while controlling —like the Chinese merchant at the next corner of the street in which I live—a capital of hundreds of thousands. This is his strength; and in our own West, through centuries, it has been the strength of the Jews.

Perhaps China can never be made to do all that Japan has done; but she will certainly be made to do what has given Japan her industrial and commercial importance. She is hemmed in by a steadily closing ring of foreign enemies : Russia north and west, France and England south, and all the sea power of the world threatening her coast. That she will be dominated is practically certain ; the doubt is, how and by whom. Russia cannot be trusted with the control of those hundreds of millions ; and a partition of Chinese territory would present many difficult problems. Very possibly she will be long allowed to retain her independence in name, after having lost it in fact. She will not be permitted to exclude foreigners from her interior during any great length of time. If she will not build railroads and establish telegraph lines, the work will be done by foreign capital, and she will have to pay for it in the end. She will be exploited as much as possible ; and, for the sake of the exploiters, foreign military power will force order, sanitary law compel cleanliness, engineering provide against catastrophes. She cannot be compelled to change her creeds or to study Western science in all her schools ; but she will have to work very hard, and to keep her cities free from plague. By remaining otherwise

158

unchanged, she will become, not less dangerous, but more dangerous.

From the most ancient times Chinese multiplication has been checked at intervals by calamities of such magnitude that, to find any parallel for them in Western history, we must recall the slaughters of the Crusaders and the ravages of the Black Death. Enormous famines, enormous inundations, frightful revolutions provoked by misery, have periodically thinned the number of China's millions. Even in our own era there have been disasters too large for the imagination to realize without difficulty. The Tai-ping rebellion cost twenty millions of lives, the later Mohammedan revolt in the West more than two million five hundred thousand; and comparatively recent famines and floods have also swept millions out of existence. But whatever Western Power rule China hereafter, that Power will have to oppose and to overcome, for reasons of self-interest, all those natural or unnatural checks upon multiplication which have hitherto kept the population at a relatively constant figure. The cholera and the plague must be conquered, the inundations must be prevented, the famines must be provided against, and infanticide must be prohibited.

As for the new political situation in the East, the guarantee of the Chinese indemnity to Japan by Russia, the rumours of a European combination to offset Russia's financial diplomacy, the possibilities of an Anglo-Japanese alliance, the supposed project for a Russian railway through Manchuria, the story of a secret Russo-Chinese compact, the state of anarchy in Korea following upon the brutal murder of the queen, the tangle of interests and the confusion of perils,—all this I confess myself utterly unable to express any opinion about. At the instant nothing appears clear except that China will be controlled, and that Japan has become a new and important factor in all international adjustments or readjustments of the balance of power in the Pacific.

## VIII

No successful attempt has yet been made, by anyone familiar with the Far East, to controvert the views of Dr Pearson. Not one of the many antagonistic reviews of his work has even yielded proof of knowledge competent to deal with his facts. Professor Huxley indeed suggested—in a short appreciative note appended to his essay, *Methods and Results of Ethnology* [1]—that future therapeutic science might find ways to render the tropics less uninhabitable for white races than Dr Pearson believed. But this suggestion does not touch the question of obstacles, more serious than fever, which a tropical climate offers to intellectual development, nor the question of race competition in temperate climates, nor any of the important social problems to which Dr Pearson called attention. Religious criticisms of the book have been numerous and hostile ; but they have contained nothing more noteworthy than the assertion that Dr Pearson's opinions were due to his want of faith in

[1] *Collected Essays*, 1894.

Providence. Such a statement amounts only to the alarming admission that we should hope for some miracle to save us from extermination. Various journalists on this side of the world have ventured the supposition that a Western domination of China might gradually force up the standard of Chinese living to such a degree as would leave Oriental competition no more to be dreaded than international competition at home; and they have cited the steady increase of the cost of life in Japan as a proof of the possibility. But even could it be shown that the cost of living in Japan is ikely, say at the close of the twentieth century, to equal the average cost of life in Europe, it were still poor reasoning to argue that the influence of Occidental civilization must necessarily produce similar results in China, under absolutely different conditions and among a people of totally opposite character. What distinguishes the Chinese race from every other civilized race is their inherent power to resist, under all imaginable circumstances, every influence calculated to raise their standard of living. The

men who best know China are just the men
who cannot conceive the possibility of raising
the standard of Chinese living to the Western
level. Eventually, under foreign domination,
the social conditions would certainly be
modified, but never so modified as to render
Chinese competition less dangerous, because
the standard of living would not be very
materially affected by any social reforms.
On the other hand, it is not difficult to
imagine conditions at home which would
rapidly force down the living-standard, and
manifest themselves later in a shrinkage of
population. That the future industrial competition between Occident and Orient must
be largely decided by physiological economy
is not to be doubted, and the period of the
greatest possible amount of human suffering
is visibly approaching. The great cause of
human suffering, and therefore of all progress in civilization, has been pressure of
population ; but the worst, as Herbert
Spencer long since pointed out, has yet
to come : " Though by the emigration that
takes place when the pressure arrives at a
certain intensity temporary relief is from

time to time obtained, yet as by this process all habitable countries must become peopled, it follows that in the end the pressure, whatever it may then be, must be borne in full."[1] In such an epoch the races of the Occident can only maintain their standard of living by forcing other races out of existence; and in the mere ability to live they will probably find themselves overmatched.

What Chinese competition would then mean cannot be imagined without a clear understanding of one ugly fact which distinguishes modern civilization in the West from ancient civilization in the Far East,— its monstrous egotism. As Professor Huxley has shown, the so-called 'struggle for existence' in Western society is not really a struggle to live, but a struggle to enjoy, and therefore something far more cruel than a contest for the right to exist.[2] According to Far-Eastern philosophy, any society founded upon such a system of selfish and sensual intercompetition is doomed to perish;

[1] *Principles of Biology,* "Human Population in the Future," vol. ii, chap. xiii.

[2] *Evolution and Ethics,* Prolegomena, xiv.

and Far-Eastern philosophy may be right.
At all events, the struggle to come will be
one between luxurious races, accustomed to
regard pleasure, at any cost, as the object
of existence, and a people of hundreds of
millions disciplined for thousands of years
to the most untiring industry and the most
self-denying thrift, under conditions which
would mean worse than death for our working
masses,—a people, in short, quite content to
strive to the uttermost in exchange for the
simple privilege of life.

Pessimistic as Dr Pearson's views seemed
to most readers at the time when his book
was first published, they now command
more attention than was accorded to them
before the late war between China and Japan.
They are forcing new convictions and new
apprehensions.  It is certain that the conditions of society in Western countries are
not now ameliorating ; and it is not difficult to believe that the decay of faith, the
substitution of conventionalism for true
religion, the ever-growing hunger of pleasure,
the constant aggravation of suffering, may be

signs of that senescence which precedes the death of a civilization. It is possible that the races of the Occident have almost exhausted their capacity for further development, and even that, as distinct races, they are doomed to disappear. Nor is it unnatural to suppose that the future will belong to the races of the Far East.

But a more optimistic view of the future is also possible. Though there be signs in Western civilization of the disintegration of existing social structures, there are signs also of new latent forces that will recreate society upon another and a more normal plan. There are unmistakable growing tendencies to international union, to the most complete industrial and commercial federation. International necessities are rapidly breaking down old prejudices and conservatisms, while developing cosmopolite feeling. The great fraternities of science and of art have declared themselves independent of country or class or creed, and recognize only the aristocracy of intellect. Few thinkers would now smile at the prediction that international war will be made impossible, or doubt the coming

166

realization of Victor Hugo's dream of the " United States of Europe." And this would signify nothing less than the final obliteration of national frontiers, the removal of all barriers between European peoples, the ultimate fusion of Western races into one vast social organism. Such fusion is even now visibly beginning. The tendency of Western civilization in its present form is to unite the strong while crushing the weak, and individual superiority seeks its affiliations irrespective of nationality.

But the promise of international coalescence in the West suggests the probability of far larger tendencies to unification in the remoter future,—to unification not of nations only, but of widely divergent races. The evolutional trend would seem to be toward universal brotherhood, without distinctions of country, creed, or blood. It is neither unscientific nor unreasonable to suppose the world eventually peopled by a race different from any now existing, yet created by the blending of the best types of all races ; uniting Western energy with Far-Eastern patience, Northern vigour with Southern

167

sensibility, the highest ethical feelings developed by all great religions with the largest mental faculties evolved by all civilizations ; speaking a single tongue composed from the richest and strongest elements of all pre-existing human speech ; and forming a society unimaginably unlike, yet also unimaginably superior to, anything which now is or has ever been.

To many the mere thought of a fusion of races will be repellent, because of ancient and powerful prejudices once essential to national self-preservation. But as a matter of scientific fact we know that none of the present higher races is really a pure race, but represents the blending, in prehistoric times, of races that have individually disappeared from the earth. All our prejudices of nationality and race and creed have doubtless had their usefulness, and some will probably continue to have usefulness for ages to be ; but the way to the highest progress can be reached only through the final extinction of all prejudice,—through the annihilation of every form of selfishness, whether individual or national or racial, that opposes itself to the evolution of the feeling of universal brotherhood. The great Harvey said, "*Our progress is from self-interest to self-annihilation.*" Modern thought endorses the truth of that utterance. But the truth itself is older by thousands of years than Harvey; for it was spoken, long before the age of Christ, by the lips of the Buddha.

# CHIN-CHIN KOBAKAMA

# CHIN-CHIN KOBAKAMA

THE floor of a Japanese room is covered with beautiful thick soft mats of woven reeds. They fit very closely together, so that you can just slip a knife-blade between them. They are changed once every year, and are kept very clean. The Japanese never wear shoes in the house, and do not use chairs or furniture such as English people use. They sit, sleep, eat, and sometimes even write upon the floor. So the mats must be kept very clean indeed, and Japanese children are taught, just as soon as they can speak, never to spoil or dirty the mats.

Now Japanese children are really very good. All travellers, who have written pleasant books about Japan, declare that Japanese children are much more obedient than English children and much less mischievous. They do not spoil and dirty things, and they do not even break their own toys. A little Japanese girl does not break her doll. No, she takes great care of it, and keeps it even after she becomes a woman and is married. When she becomes a mother, and has a daughter, she gives the doll to that little daughter. And the child takes the same care of the doll that her mother did, and preserves it until she grows up, and gives it at last to her own children, who play with it just as nicely as their grandmother did. So I,—who am writing this little story for you,—have seen in Japan, dolls more than a hundred years old, looking just as pretty as when they were new. This will show you how very good Japanese children are ; and you will be able to understand why the floor of a Japanese room is nearly always kept clean,—not scratched and spoiled by mischievous play.

You ask me whether all, *all* Japanese children are as good as that? Well—no, there are a few, a very few naughty ones. And what happens to the mats in the houses of these naughty children? Nothing very bad—because there are fairies who take care of the mats. These fairies tease and frighten children who dirty or spoil the mats. At least—they used to tease and frighten such mischievous children. I am not quite sure whether those little fairies still live in Japan,—

because the new railways and the telegraph-poles have frightened a great many fairies away. But here is a little story about them :

Once there was a little girl who was very pretty, but also very lazy. Her parents were rich, and had a great many servants ; and these servants were very fond of the little girl, and did everything for her which she ought to have been able to do for herself. Perhaps this was what made her so lazy. When she grew up into a beautiful woman, she still remained lazy ; but as the servants always dressed and undressed her, and arranged her hair, she looked very charming, and nobody thought about her faults.

At last she was married to a brave warrior, and went away with him to live in another house where there were but few servants. She was sorry not to have as many servants as she had had at home, because she was obliged to do several things for herself, which other folks had always done for her. It was such trouble to her to dress herself, and take care of her own clothes, and keep herself looking neat and pretty to please her husband. But as he was a warrior, and often had to be far away from home with the army, she could sometimes be just as lazy as she wished. Her husband's parents were very old and good-natured, and never scolded her.

Well, one night while her husband was away with the army, she was awakened by queer little noises in her room. By the light of a big paper-lantern she could see very well ; and she saw strange things. What ?

Hundreds of little men, dressed just like Japanese warriors, but only about one inch high, were dancing all round her pillow. They wore the same kind of dress her husband wore on holidays (*Kamishimo*, a long robe with square shoulders), and their hair was tied up in knots, and each wore two tiny swords. They all looked at her as they danced, and laughed, and they all sang the same song, over and over again :

> " *Chin-chin Kobakama,*
> *Yomo fuké sōro,*
> *Oshizumare, Hime-gimi !*
> *Ya ton ton !* "

Which meant : " We are the Chin-chin

Kobakama ; the hour is late ; sleep, honour-
able, noble darling ! ''

The words seemed very polite ; but she
soon saw that the little men were only
making cruel fun of her. They also made
ugly faces at her.

She tried to catch some of them ; but
they jumped about so quickly that she could
not. Then she tried to drive them away ;
but they would not go, and they never
stopped singing

*" Chin-chin Kobakama,"*

and laughing at her. Then she knew they
were little fairies, and became so frightened
that she could not even cry out. They
danced around her until morning; then they
all vanished suddenly.

She was ashamed to tell anybody what had
happened—because, as she was the wife of a
warrior, she did not wish anybody to know
how frightened she had been.

Next night, again the little men came and
danced, and they came also the night after
that, and every night—always at the same
hour, which the old Japanese used to call the

M

'Hour of the Ox'; that is, about two o'clock in the morning by our time. At last she became very sick, through want of sleep and through fright. But the little men would not leave her alone.

When her husband came back home, he was very sorry to find her sick in bed. At first she was afraid to tell him what had made her ill, for fear that he would laugh at her. But he was so kind, and coaxed her so gently, that after a while she told him what happened every night.

He did not laugh at her at all, but looked very serious for a time. Then he asked :

" At what time do they come ? "

She answered : " Always at the same hour —the ' Hour of the Ox.' "

" Very well," said her husband, " to-night I shall hide and watch for them. Do not be frightened."

So that night the warrior hid himself in a closet in the sleeping room, and kept watch through a chink between the sliding doors.

He waited and watched until the ' Hour of the Ox.' Then, all at once, the little men

178

came up through the mats, and began their dance and their song :

> " *Chin-chin Kobakama,*
> *Yomo fuké sŏro.*"

They looked so queer, and danced in such a funny way, that the warrior could scarcely keep from laughing. But he saw his young wife's frightened face ; and then remembering that nearly all Japanese ghosts and goblins are afraid of a sword, he drew his blade, and rushed out of the closet, and struck at the little dancers. Immediately they all turned into—what do you think ?

> *Toothpicks !*

There were no more little warriors—only a lot of old toothpicks scattered over the mats.

The young wife had been too lazy to put her toothpicks away properly ; and every day, after having used a new toothpick, she would stick it down between the mats on the floor, to get rid of it. So the little fairies who take care of the floor-mats became angry with her, and tormented her.

Her husband scolded her, and she was so ashamed that she did not know what to do. A servant was called, and the toothpicks were taken away and burned. After that the little men never came back again.

There is also a story told about a lazy little girl, who used to eat plums, and afterwards hide the plum-stones between the floor-mats. For a long time she was able to do this without being found out. But at last the fairies got angry and punished her.

For every night, tiny, tiny women—all wearing bright red robes with very long sleeves,—rose up from the floor at the same hour, and danced, and made faces at her and prevented her from sleeping.

Her mother one night sat up to watch, and saw them, and struck at them,—and they all turned into plum-stones ! So the naughtiness of that little girl was found out. After that she became a very good girl indeed.

# THE GOBLIN-SPIDER

# THE GOBLIN-SPIDER

IN very ancient books it is said that there used to be many goblin-spiders in Japan.

Some folks declare there are still some goblin-spiders. During the daytime they look just like common spiders; but very late at night, when everybody is asleep, and there is no sound, they become very, very big, and do awful things. Goblin-spiders are supposed also to have the magical power of taking human shape—so as to deceive people. And there is a famous Japanese story about such a spider.

There was once, in some lonely part of the country, a haunted temple. No one could live in the building because of the goblins that had taken possession of it. Many brave samurai went to that place at various times for the purpose of killing the goblins. But they were never heard of again after they had entered the temple.

At last one who was famous for his courage and his prudence, went to the temple to watch during the night. And he said to those who accompanied him there: " If in the morning

I be still alive, I shall drum upon the drum of the temple." Then he was left alone, to watch by the light of a lamp.

As the night advanced he crouched down under the altar, which supported a dusty image of Buddha. He saw nothing strange and heard no sound till after midnight. Then there came a goblin, having but half a body and one eye, and said : *"Hitokusai!"* (There is the smell of a man.) But the samurai did not move. The goblin went away.

Then there came a priest and played upon a *samisen* so wonderfully that the samurai felt sure it was not the playing of a man. So he leaped up with his sword drawn. The priest, seeing him, burst out laughing, and said : " So you thought I was a goblin? Oh, no ! I am only the priest of this temple ; but I have to play to keep off the goblins. Does not this *samisen* sound well ? Please play a little."

And he offered the instrument to the samurai, who grasped it very cautiously with his left hand. But instantly the *samisen* changed into a monstrous spider-web, and
184

the priest into a goblin-spider; and the warrior found himself caught fast in the web, by the left hand. He struggled bravely, and struck at the spider with his sword, and wounded it; but he soon became entangled still more in the net, and could not move.

However, the wounded spider crawled away, and the sun rose. In a little while the people came and found the samurai in the horrible web, and freed him. They saw tracks of blood upon the floor, and followed the tracks out of the temple to a hole in the deserted garden. Out of the hole issued a frightful sound of groaning. They found the wounded goblin in the hole, and killed it.

# THE OLD WOMAN WHO LOST HER DUMPLING

# THE OLD WOMAN WHO LOST HER DUMPLING

LONG, long ago there was a funny old woman, who liked to laugh and to make dumplings of rice-flour.

One day, while she was preparing some dumplings for dinner, she let one fall; and it rolled into a hole in the earthen floor of her little kitchen and disappeared. The old woman tried to reach it by putting her hand down the hole, and all at once the earth gave way, and the old woman fell in.

She fell quite a distance, but was not a bit hurt; and when she got up on her feet again, she saw that she was standing on a road, just like the road before her house. It was quite light down there; and she could see plenty of rice-fields, but no one in them. How all this happened, I cannot tell you. But it seems that the old woman had fallen into another country.

The road she had fallen upon sloped very much: so, after having looked for her dumpling in vain, she thought that it must have rolled farther away down the slope. She ran down the road to look, crying:

" My dumpling, my dumpling ! Where is that dumpling of mine ? "

After a little while she saw a stone *Fizō* standing by the roadside, and she said :

" O Lord *Fizō*, did you see my dumpling ? "

*Fizō* answered :

" Yes, I saw your dumpling rolling by me down the road. But you had better not go any farther, because there is a wicked *Oni* living down there, who eats people."

But the old woman only laughed, and ran on farther down the road, crying : " My dumpling, my dumpling ! Where is that dumpling of mine ? "

And she came to another statue of *Fizō*, and asked it :

" O kind Lord *Fizō*, did you see my dumpling ? "

And *Fizō* said :

" Yes, I saw your dumpling go by a little while ago. But you must not run any farther, because there is a wicked *Oni* down there, who eats people."

But she only laughed, and ran on, still crying out : " My dumpling, my dumpling ! Where is that dumpling of mine ? "

190

And she came to a third *Fizō*, and asked it :

" O dear Lord *Fizō*, did you see my dumpling ? "

But *Fizō* said :

" Don't talk about your dumpling now. Here is the *Oni* coming. Squat down here behind my sleeve, and don't make any noise."

Presently the *Oni* came very close, and stopped and bowed to *Fizō*, and said :

" Good-day, *Fizō San* ! "

*Fizō* said good-day, too, very politely.

Then the *Oni* suddenly snuffed the air two or three times in a suspicious way, and cried out :

" *Fizō San, Fizō San* ! I smell a smell of mankind somewhere—don't you ? "

" Oh ! " said *Fizō*, " perhaps you are mistaken."

" No, no ! " said the *Oni* after snuffing the air again, " I smell a smell of mankind."

Then the old woman could not help laughing—" *Te-he-he* ! "—and the *Oni* immediately reached down his big hairy hand behind *Fizō's* sleeve, and pulled her out, still laughing, " *Te-he-he* ! "

191

" Ah ! ha ! " cried the *Oni*.

Then *Fizō* said :

" What are you going to do with that good old woman ?  You must not hurt her."

" I won't," said the *Oni*.   " But I will take her home with me to cook for us."

" *Te-he-he !* " laughed the old woman.

" Very well," said *Fizō* ;  " but you must really be kind to her.   If you are not I shall be very angry."

" I won't hurt her at all," promised the *Oni* ;  " and she will only have to do a little work for us every day. Good-bye, *Fizō San.*"

Then the *Oni* took the old woman far down the road, till they came to a wide deep river, where there was a boat.   He put her into the boat, and took her across the river to his house.   It was a very large house.   He led her at once into the kitchen, and told her to cook some dinner for himself and the other *Oni* who lived with him.   And he gave her a small wooden rice-paddle, and said :

" You must always put only one grain of rice into the pot, and when you stir that one grain of rice in the water with this paddle, the grain will multiply until the pot is full."

So the old woman put just one rice-grain into the pot, as the *Oni* told her, and began to stir it with the paddle ; and, as she stirred, the one grain became two,—then four,—then eight,—then sixteen, thirty-two, sixty-four, and so on. Every time she moved the paddle the rice increased in quantity ; and in a few minutes the great pot was full.

After that, the funny old woman stayed a long time in the house of the *Oni*, and every day cooked food for him and for all his friends. The *Oni* never hurt or frightened her, and her work was made quite easy by the magic paddle—although she had to cook a very, very great quantity of rice, because an *Oni* eats much more than any human being eats.

But she felt lonely, and always wished very much to go back to her own little house, and make her dumplings. And one day, when the *Oni* were all out somewhere, she thought she would try to run away.

She first took the magic paddle, and slipped it under her girdle ; and then she went down to the river. No one saw her; and the boat was there. She got into it, and pushed off; and as she could row very well, she was soon far away from the shore.

But the river was very wide; and she had not rowed more than one-fourth of the way across, when the *Oni*, all of them, came back to the house.

They found that their cook was gone, and the magic paddle, too. They ran down to the river at once, and saw the old woman rowing away very fast.

Perhaps they could not swim: at all events they had no boat; and they thought the only way they could catch the funny old woman would be to drink up all the water of the river before she got to the other bank. So they knelt down, and began to drink so fast that before the old woman had got half way over, the water had become quite low.

But the old woman kept on rowing until the water had got so shallow that the *Oni* stopped drinking, and began to wade across. Then she dropped her oar, took the magic paddle from her girdle, and shook it at the

*Oni,* and made such funny faces that the *Oni* all burst out laughing.

But the moment they laughed, they could not help throwing up all the water they had drunk, and so the river became full again. The *Oni* could not cross ; and the funny old woman got safely over to the other side, and ran away up the road as fast as she could.

She never stopped running until she found herself at home again.

After that she was very happy ; for she could make dumplings whenever she pleased. Besides, she had the magic paddle to make rice for her. She sold her dumplings to her neighbours and passengers, and in quite a short time she became rich.

# THE BOY WHO DREW
CATS

# THE BOY WHO DREW CATS

A LONG, long time ago, in a small country village in Japan, there lived a poor farmer and his wife, who were very good people. They had a number of children, and found it very hard to feed them all. The elder son was strong enough when only fourteen years old to help his father; and the little girls learned to help their mother almost as soon as they could walk.

But the youngest child, a little boy, did not seem to be fit for hard work. He was very clever,—cleverer than all his brothers and sisters; but he was quite weak and small, and people said he could never grow very big. So his parents thought it would be better for him to become a priest than to become a farmer. They took him with them to the village temple one day, and asked the good old priest who lived there, if he would have their little boy for his acolyte, and teach him all that a priest ought to know.

The old man spoke kindly to the lad, and asked him some hard questions. So clever

199

were the answers that the priest agreed to take the little fellow into the temple as an acolyte, and to educate him for the priesthood.

The boy learned quickly what the old priest told him, and was very obedient in most things. But he had one fault. He liked to draw cats during study hours, and to draw cats even where cats ought not to have been drawn at all.

Whenever he found himself alone, he drew cats. He drew them on the margins of the priest's books, and on all the screens of the temple, and on the walls, and on the pillars. Several times the priest told him this was not right ; but he did not stop drawing cats. He drew them because he could not really help it. He had what is called ' the genius of an *artist*,' and just for that reason he was not quite fit to be an acolyte ;—a good acolyte should study books.

One day after he had drawn some very clever pictures of cats upon a paper screen, the old priest said to him severely : " My boy, you must go away from this temple at once. You will never make a good priest, but perhaps you will become a great artist. Now let me give you a last piece of advice, and be sure you never forget it. *Avoid large places at night ;—keep to small !* "

The boy did not know what the priest meant by saying, " *Avoid large places ;—keep to small.*" He thought and thought, while he was tying up his little bundle of clothes to go away ; but he could not understand those words, and he was afraid to speak to the priest any more, except to say good-bye.

He left the temple very sorrowfully, and began to wonder what he should do. If he went straight home he felt sure his father would punish him for having been disobedient to the priest : so he was afraid to go home. All at once he remembered that at the next village, twelve miles away, there was a very big temple. He had heard there were several priests at that temple ; and he made up his mind to go to them and ask them to take him for their acolyte.

Now that big temple was closed up, but the boy did not know this fact. The reason it had been closed up was that a goblin had frightened the priests away, and had taken possession of the place. Some brave warriors had afterwards gone to the temple at night to kill the goblin ; but they had never been seen alive again. Nobody had ever told these things to the boy ;—so he walked all the way to the village hoping to be kindly treated by the priests.

When he got to the village it was already dark, and all the people were in bed ; but he saw the big temple on a hill at the other end of the principal street, and he saw there was a light in the temple. People who tell the story say the goblin used to make that light, in order to tempt lonely travellers to ask for shelter. The boy went at once to the temple, and knocked. There was no sound inside. He knocked and knocked again ; but still nobody came. At last he pushed gently at the door, and was quite glad to find that it had not been fastened. So he went in, and saw a lamp burning,—but no priest.

He thought some priest would be sure to come very soon, and he sat down and waited. Then he noticed that everything in the temple was grey with dust, and thickly spun over with cobwebs. So he thought to himself that the priests would certainly like to have an acolyte, to keep the place clean. He wondered why they had allowed everything to get so dusty. What most pleased him, however, were some big white screens, good to paint cats upon. Though he was tired, he looked at once for a writing box, and found one, and ground some ink, and began to paint cats.

He painted a great many cats upon the screens; and then he began to feel very, very sleepy. He was just on the point of lying down to sleep beside one of the screens, when he suddenly remembered the words, " *Avoid large places ;—keep to small !* "

The temple was very large; he was all alone; and as he thought of these words,— though he could not quite understand them —he began to feel for the first time a little afraid; and he resolved to look for a *small place* in which to sleep. He found a little cabinet, with a sliding door, and went into it, and shut himself up. Then he lay down and fell fast asleep.

Very late in the night he was awakened by

a most terrible noise,—a noise of fighting and screaming. It was so dreadful that he was afraid even to look through a chink of the little cabinet : he lay very still, holding his breath for fright.

The light that had been in the temple went out ; but the awful sounds continued, and became more awful, and all the temple shook. After a long time silence came ; but the boy was still afraid to move. He did not move until the light of the morning sun shone into the cabinet through the chinks of the little door.

Then he got out of his hiding-place very cautiously, and looked about. The first thing he saw was that all the floor of the temple was covered with blood. And then he saw, lying dead in the middle of it, an enormous, monstrous rat,—a goblin-rat, —bigger than a cow !

But who or what could have killed it ? There was no man or other creature to be seen. Suddenly the boy observed that the mouths of all the cats he had drawn the night before, were red and wet with blood. Then he knew that the goblin had been killed by the cats which he had drawn.   And then also, for the first time, he understood why the wise old priest had said to him, " *Avoid large places at night ;—keep to small.*"

Afterward that boy became a very famous artist.   Some of the cats which he drew are still shown to travellers in Japan.

2

# ImTheStory.com

Personalized Classic Books in many genre's

Unique gift for kids, partners, friends, colleagues

Customize:

- Character Names
- Upload your own front/back cover images (optional)
- Inscribe a personal message/dedication on the
  inside page (optional)

Customize many titles Including

- Alice in Wonderland
- Romeo and Juliet
- The Wizard of Oz
- A Christmas Carol
- Dracula
- Dr. Jekyll & Mr. Hyde
- And more...

Lightning Source UK Ltd.
Milton Keynes UK
UKHW02f2036110418
320904UK00008B/299/P